MIND Diet for Two

MIND DIET FOR TWO

65 Perfectly Portioned Recipes to Boost Your Brain Health

Laura Ali, MS, RDN, LDN

ROCKRIDGE
PRESS

Interior and Cover Designer: Erik Jacobsen
Art Producer: Sara Feinstein
Editor: Sierra Machado
Production Editor: Jax Berman
Production Manager: David Zapanta

Cover photography © 2021 Laura Flippen. Cover food styling by Laura Flippen. Interior photography © Hélène Dujardin, p. ii, vi, 60, 76; Nadine Greeff, p. x; Darren Muir, p. 18, 30, 104; Andrew Purcell, p. 42; Stocksy, p. 92. Illustration © Steve Mack, p. v. All other illustration used under license from Shutterstock.

Paperback ISBN: 978-1-63878-376-3
eBook ISBN: 978-1-63878-527-9
R0

To Mark, my cheerleader, taste tester, and dishwasher.
Thank you for always believing in me!

Contents

Introduction

I've always loved cooking. A delicious meal has a magical ability to bring people together and evoke memories of special times, and, for me, it is something I want my friends and family to enjoy and savor. As a registered dietitian, I also understand the various ways food can affect our health.

Over the past 30 years, I've researched and explored the role that food plays in reducing the risk of heart disease, diabetes, and some cancers. I've also extensively studied how food affects our brain health—both now and as we age. I find it incredibly inspiring to share simple and empowering ways to eat every day to support brain health, and that's why I wrote this book.

The MIND diet is a combination of two of the most highly regarded diets for long-term health: the Mediterranean diet and the DASH (Dietary Approaches to Stop Hypertension) diet. The two components of the MIND diet are reducing sodium intake and following a plant-focused eating plan that incorporates whole grains, vegetables, fruit, seafood, and nuts.

Unfortunately, my husband and I both have a family history of Alzheimer's disease, and we have watched some of our close relatives suffer with dementia. We have always followed a Mediterranean-style diet, but as we get older, it has become more important to us than ever to incorporate meals that are MIND diet friendly into our routine. We eat a lot of vegetables, whole grains, and seafood, and we enjoy a glass of wine while reconnecting after a long day.

Whether you are meal planning with your partner, a roommate, or a family member, cooking for only two people can present challenges. Most recipes and package sizes are geared toward families, so you often end up having to throw away uneaten leftovers. That is also why I felt inspired to write this book: to design recipes specifically tailored for two.

Many of the recipes in this book use a few of the same ingredients in creative ways to minimize food waste, but they also provide enough variety to prevent you from feeling like you are eating the same things over and over. Most of the recipes make two servings, and you'll find tips and tricks for shopping and meal planning for two.

This book features 65 recipes, including quick breakfasts, simple lunches, and satisfying dinners, all using ingredients that are encouraged on the MIND diet. There are many plant-based meals, seafood dishes, and snacks and desserts that incorporate nuts, berries, and whole grains. For special occasions, I have included a few indulgent dishes that still follow MIND diet principles. And you'll discover a handful of recipes, such as soups and stews, that make more than two portions and freeze easily. (It's nice to have a few healthy dishes in the freezer to pull out on a busy weeknight!)

My hope is that by providing a wide variety of recipes that support brain health and are designed for two, it will become easier for you and your loved one to make the MIND diet a part of your lives.

CHAPTER 1

The Power of the MIND Diet

Alzheimer's disease and dementia affect more than 50 million people worldwide. It's devastating for not only the person experiencing it but also their family and caregivers. As we learn more about Alzheimer's and potential causes of dementia, it has become clear that making simple changes to what you eat and how you live may make a difference.

Boost Your Brain Health, Together

This book is designed to help you discover a delicious way of eating and living that will help support brain health with recipes specifically designed for two. Whether two means you and a partner, roommate, friend, or family member who is experiencing cognitive decline, knowing you have the power to support your brain health together through the food you eat can be life changing.

Although some things are beyond your control, such as family history and genetics, simple lifestyle changes have the potential to improve your brain health and possibly delay the onset of mental decline. The food we eat presents one of the biggest opportunities to positively affect our brains. Two great examples are blueberries and fish. Blueberries contain some of the highest levels of antioxidants of all fruits and vegetables. Several studies have shown that people who eat blueberries at least once a week have an improvement in their memory and experience slower cognitive decline. Seafood, especially fish that are rich in omega-3 fatty acids, has been associated with a lower risk of developing dementia, including Alzheimer's disease. One serving a week of fatty fish is recommended on the MIND diet. Salmon, trout, and tuna are especially good choices because they are great sources of omega-3 fatty acids.

Just as there are foods that have a protective effect, eating too much of others may negatively affect brain health. Studies show that people who eat foods high in refined sugar and saturated fats, such as pastries, baked goods, and fried foods, have an increase in harmful amyloid plaque buildup in the brain. Although the MIND diet doesn't require you eliminate these foods, it encourages you to limit them.

Whether you are cooking for yourself and your significant other or making meals for other family members, these recipes will feed two people and incorporate the foods recommended on the MIND diet.

What Is the MIND Diet?

The MIND diet, or the Mediterranean-DASH Intervention for Neurodegenerative Delay diet, is a combination of two of the healthiest diets in the world—the Mediterranean diet and the DASH (Dietary Approaches to Stop Hypertension) diet—and the research on its effect on brain health is incredibly promising.

The Mediterranean diet is based on the way people in that region have eaten for centuries. It focuses on plant-based foods and whole grains while incorporating healthy fats (such as those found in olive oil, seafood, and nuts) along with dairy and wine. The DASH diet similarly focuses on nutrient-rich foods (known to help with blood pressure control), healthy fats, and low-fat dairy, but it also encourages a reduction in sodium intake. Both the Mediterranean and DASH diets have shown promise in their ability to slow or delay the onset of cognitive decline.

Researchers at Rush University in Chicago tested the MIND diet along with the Mediterranean and DASH diets with healthy elderly residents. They found all three diets, when adhered to strictly, showed a delay in cognitive aging, but those following the MIND diet showed a significant delay in the slowing of cognitive abilities and a 53 percent reduction in the risk of developing Alzheimer's disease. What was most impressive was even those who only moderately followed the MIND diet saw a 35 percent reduced risk of developing the disease. Neither of the other two diets produced this result.

What sets the MIND diet apart is that it's the first eating plan that focuses on foods that specifically support and improve cognitive health. Although plant foods overall are the focus, the MIND diet specifically hones in on 10 types of food that should be eaten regularly: berries, leafy greens, vegetables, whole grains, nuts and seeds, beans, legumes, fish, poultry, and olive oil (used for cooking). Five types of foods should be limited: pastries, red meat, cheese, fried food and fast food, and butter or margarine.

As a registered dietitian who has watched family members struggle with dementia and friends care for relatives with cognitive decline, I find the research behind the MIND diet encouraging. It just makes sense. Many of the same principles people are instructed to follow to prevent or reduce the risk of heart disease, cancer, and other chronic diseases are included in the MIND diet.

The Nutrients Your Brain Needs to Thrive

As the mass communication system that sends signals to all parts of your body, the brain is one of our most important organs. It regulates everything we do—from eating, sleeping, and thinking to how quickly our hearts beat, and how and when we move.

Scientists have found that people with Alzheimer's disease have plaque buildup and amyloid protein clusters throughout the brain. These barriers cause the communication system to short-circuit and interfere with the brain's messages to the body, impacting the ability to learn and remember. These barriers also interfere with coordination, movement, and the ability to perform daily activities, as well as mood and personality. Preserving this delicate system and keeping the lines of communication open is what the MIND diet is all about, and certain nutrients play critical roles:

Flavonoids: Flavonoids are the components in plants that provide their brilliant colors. There are more than 6,000 known flavonoids found in fruits, vegetables, tea, cocoa, and wine, and all contain antioxidant and anti-inflammatory properties. They protect the body's cells from damage (think of a protective coat of polyurethane on a piece of wood) and reduce inflammation. Recent research has also suggested that flavonoids may inhibit the buildup of amyloid proteins in the brain.

Carotenoids: Carotenoids are the compounds in plants that add the red, yellow, and orange colors. They have strong antioxidant and anti-inflammatory properties. Tomatoes, carrots, sweet potatoes, and winter squash, like acorn or butternut squash, are all examples of foods rich in carotenoids.

B vitamins: Elevated levels of homocysteine (an amino acid produced when proteins are broken down) have been identified as a marker for a risk of dementia. High homocysteine levels are also an indication of poor vitamin B levels, specifically folate, vitamin B6, and vitamin B12. Whole grains and animal products such as seafood, beef, and chicken are good sources of B vitamins.

Omega-3 fatty acids: Omega-3 fatty acids are a group of unsaturated fats found primarily in seafood, nuts, and seeds. The omega-3 fatty acid DHA is found in the brain and has anti-inflammatory properties. Some evidence suggests that DHA helps reduce the formation of amyloid protein clusters.

Choline: Choline helps the brain communicate with other parts of the body. It also helps maintain cell structure and may play a role in the growth and development of the brain, specifically the areas responsible for learning, memory, mood, and behavior. Choline is found in eggs, vegetables, and grains.

Minerals: Magnesium, potassium, and calcium are minerals found in fruits and vegetables, nuts, beans, and whole grains. They help with energy production, muscle contraction, blood flow to the brain, and blood pressure management.

What to Eat on the MIND Diet

The MIND diet focuses on foods and nutrients that have been shown to reduce plaque buildup, amyloid protein tangles, and inflammation in the brain. Here's a breakdown of the supportive foods to consume, as well as those to limit.

MIND Superfoods to Love

Leafy greens: Rich in vitamin K, carotenoids, B vitamins, potassium, and fiber, leafy greens—such as kale, spinach, Swiss chard, arugula, and romaine—have been shown to have powerful effects on cognitive health. Enjoy a salad with dinner, mix some greens into pasta, or add them to scrambled eggs or even smoothies.

CHOOSE MIND-FUL HABITS

Like the Mediterranean diet, the MIND diet involves both healthy food and lifestyle choices. Our lifestyles impact our health as much as our food intake does.

Avoid (or quit) smoking. Smoking is associated with several chronic diseases and has been linked to cognitive decline. Some research suggests that the area of the brain responsible for language and memory is thinner in smokers than nonsmokers. One of the best things you can do for your brain and your overall health is to quit smoking and encourage your family members to do the same.

Get adequate and restful sleep. While we sleep, brain cells regenerate, keeping the communication pathways in the brain open. Tips for restful sleep include turning off electronics one hour before bedtime, avoiding caffeine and alcohol late in the day, and sticking with a regular bedtime routine.

Exercise daily. Moving your body increases blood flow to your brain. Exercise may stimulate the growth of new connections between the cells responsible for communication. Plus, taking a break and moving can help the mind refocus and recharge; it can also help improve your mood.

Practice stress-reduction techniques. Chronic stress has been shown to increase cortisol levels in the brain, which leads to poor memory and visual perception. A daily practice of meditation with deep breathing, stretching, or journaling is an easy way to help reduce stress.

Other vegetables: Deep-colored vegetables such as squash, carrots, tomatoes, eggplant, summer squash, asparagus, and peas are rich in carotenoids.

Whole grains: Believe the hype: whole grains are better for you than refined ones! Use brown or wild rice in place of white, make a sandwich with multigrain bread, and add grains like barley and quinoa to your meals.

Nuts and seeds: Nuts and seeds are a delicious way to add some crunch to your salads, entrées, or afternoon snacks, and they provide protein, antioxidants, and healthy unsaturated fats, all of which are essential for brain health.

MIND Foods to Eat Regularly

Although the MIND diet is plant based, it is not a vegetarian diet. Most of the meals emphasize plants with lean protein as an accompaniment.

Berries: The research on berries and brain health is so promising, plus berries are delicious, which makes them one of my favorite parts of this diet! All types of berries are included, but blueberries and strawberries are the most beneficial for brain health. Toss some berries in with your oatmeal in the morning, add them to pancakes, or even use them to make a delicious barbecue sauce (see page 90).

Seafood: Rich in omega-3 fatty acids, fattier seafood such as salmon, sardines, tuna, and trout play an important role in brain health. Other types of seafood, including shellfish, are good sources of lean protein, minerals like iron and selenium, and B vitamins.

Beans and legumes: Full of fiber and lean protein, dried beans and legumes are an integral part of the MIND diet and are easy to add to meals and snacks. Cannellini beans, black beans, kidney beans, chickpeas, and lentils can all be added to salads, stews, or grain dishes.

Eggs: Eggs are an excellent source of protein; the yolk is a rich source of lutein, and eggs contain choline, which has important brain health properties.

Low-Fat Dairy: Products including low-fat milk, yogurt, and kefir can be a healthy part of the MIND diet. While there is limited evidence for their brain-boosting benefits, these foods are excellent sources of calcium, vitamin D, potassium, and protein.

Olive oil: Olive oil is rich in monounsaturated fats and has been shown to help reduce inflammation. I love it for its rich, fruity flavor. It is wonderful drizzled over a salad or as a dipping sauce for bread. When cooking at high temps, use avocado or grapeseed oil instead, both of which are also high in monounsaturated fats.

Foods to Limit and Avoid

Unlike so many of the popular diets today, the MIND diet doesn't eliminate any food or group of food, which is why this way of eating is so easy. It's flexible and allows for treats here and there. With that said, some foods that are high in saturated fat, trans fat, sodium, or sugar should be limited.

Red meat: Lean red meat provides protein and essential B vitamins, but aim for no more than four servings per week, and limit high-fat cuts, such as prime rib, strip steaks, and short ribs. A few recipes in this book use lean cuts of beef, pork, and lamb combined with hearty grains and vegetables (see chapter 6).

Fried and fast food: Sometimes you just can't avoid it; you're in a hurry, traveling, or just plain busy and swing by the drive-through. But try to keep fried and fast foods to no more than one serving per week, and stick with grilled items or salads when eating out.

Butter and margarine: High in saturated fat and hydrogenated oils, butter and margarine should be limited to no more than a tablespoon per day. You will find a little butter in some of the dessert and breakfast recipes, but for the most part, olive oil is the main fat used in this book.

Cheese: This is the hardest for me to limit! I love cheese, but because it is high in saturated fat and sodium, you'll want to limit it to one serving per week. A few recipes in this book include a little cheese if it imparts just the right flavor or is a classic element of a dish.

Pastries and refined sugar: Sweet treats are delicious and okay to enjoy occasionally, but they are often full of saturated fat, sodium, and sugar, and they contain few nutrients. But never fear, I've included some desserts that are MIND diet friendly and can help satisfy your sweet tooth!

MIND Diet Servings Chart

FOOD	SERVINGS PER DAY/WEEK	SERVING SIZES
Whole grains	3 servings per day	½ cup cooked whole grains; 1 cup cooked whole-grain pasta; 1 slice whole-grain bread
Leafy greens	6 servings per week	½ cup cooked; 1 cup raw
Other vegetables	At least 1 serving per day	½ cup cooked; 1 cup raw
Berries	2 to 3 servings per week	½ cup
Eggs	4 to 7 servings per week	1 egg
Beans and legumes	3 or more servings per week	½ cup cooked
Nuts and seeds	1 serving per day	1 ounce or 2 tablespoons of nut butter
Seafood	At least 1 serving per week	3 to 5 ounces
Poultry and lean meats	2 servings per week	3 ounces
Olive oil	Daily/main cooking oil	1 to 2 tablespoons
Red wine	1 serving per day	5 ounces
Butter and margarine	1 serving per day	1 tablespoon
Cheese	No more than 1 serving per week	1 ounce
Red meat	No more than 4 servings per week	3 to 5 ounces
Pastries and sweets	No more than 4 servings per week	

Shop Smart for Two

Grocery shopping for two people can be challenging. Retailers and manufacturers package items for families of four or more, so finding small quantities can be tough. Here are a few tricks for shopping for two that will help you limit food waste and save money in the long run.

- **Bring a list.** You'll be less likely to pick up things you don't need.

- **Shop from the bulk bins.** It probably sounds counterintuitive, but the bulk area is a great place for buying just the right amount, which will help you avoid having a pantry full of partially used items. If a recipe calls for ¼ cup, for example, you can buy just ¼ cup this way.

- **Don't ignore the center of the store.** Have you ever heard that you should shop only the perimeter of the store? Although this advice is well-intentioned, the center of the store is where you find many pantry staples that are important for the MIND diet, such as quinoa, oats, brown rice, and canned beans, so don't ignore it!

- **Buy large quantities occasionally.** Frozen vegetables and fruits are nice to keep on hand because you can use just what you need and store the rest. You'll likely use these foods often, so it's good to have a few from which to choose. Nuts also last when stored in the freezer, so go ahead and buy extra when they're on sale.

- **Buy meat and seafood at the meat counter.** You can buy two salmon fillets or two pork chops rather than a large package of them.

- **Stock up on certain sale items.** This works well for canned goods such as beans, tomatoes, and vegetables. For fresh items, stick with just what you need for the week.

- **Buy smaller sizes of condiments and specialty items whenever possible.** The larger size might be less expensive, but if it sits in the refrigerator and expires before you can use it, you will have wasted all the money you thought you were saving.

Plan Perfectly Portioned Meals

Meal prepping for two can take practice, and you will find that planning ahead is key. The more organized you are, the more time and money you'll save, while also minimizing food waste.

Most of the recipes in this book make two servings, but you can easily double them if you prefer to make extra and have leftovers. I often do this so I have a quick dinner ready to go on a busy day.

- Consider making meals that have common ingredients to lessen food waste. For instance, if you want to make eggplant lasagna but know you won't use the whole eggplant, plan to make a ratatouille or other eggplant-based dish to ensure you use the rest.

- Many people plan theme nights, like Taco Tuesday or Pasta Night. You can do the same for a week or a couple of days in a row. One week could be Italian inspired, for example, and the next can feature Asian or southwestern flavors. You'll use many of the same ingredients this way, and you can prep ahead to make mealtime easier and faster.

- Always look in the refrigerator, freezer, and pantry to see what you have on hand that could make a meal. If you are missing a key ingredient, add it to your shopping list. This habit will keep you from buying items you may not need.

- Cook a large batch of grains and use it multiple times during the week. For example, you can cook a pot of brown rice on Sunday, plan a rice bowl for a lunch that week, enjoy a stir-fry or curry for a dinner, and use the rest in stuffed peppers or in a salad.

A 7-Day Sample Menu

	BREAKFAST	LUNCH	DINNER
MONDAY	Blueberry Smoothie (page 21)	Hummus and Vegetable Wrap (page 41)	Honey-Mustard Salmon (page 63) with asparagus
TUESDAY	Overnight Oats with Strawberries and Almonds (page 22)	Orange Quinoa-Chickpea Salad (page 38)	Chickpea Pasta Primavera (page 50)
WEDNESDAY	Blueberry Smoothie (page 21)	Tossed salad with salmon and whole-grain bread	Stuffed Banana Peppers (page 53)
THURSDAY	Whole-grain toast with a hard-boiled egg and apple slices	Tuscan Bean Soup (page 34) with crackers	Chicken Shawarma with Couscous Salad (page 82)
FRIDAY	Overnight Oats with Strawberries and Almonds (page 22)	Hummus and Vegetable Wrap (page 41)	Eggplant with Tahini Dressing (page 46)
SATURDAY	Scrambled egg with whole-grain toast and berries	Lettuce wraps with chopped vegetables and chickpeas with Tahini Dressing (page 107)	Grilled Pork Chops with Blueberry Barbecue Sauce (page 90)
SUNDAY	Triple-Berry Mini Dutch Baby (page 24)	Tossed salad with chickpeas, quinoa, avocado, and whole-grain bread	Stuffed Flounder with Grain Salad (page 73)

Set Up Your MIND Kitchen for Two

Cooking for two may mean changing up some of the staples you keep in the kitchen. It's important to have some items always available in the pantry, refrigerator, and freezer so you can pull a meal together quickly. You'll find there are common ingredients throughout this book that you'll use over and over, so they are good to keep on hand.

Pantry and Counter

Whole grains: Quinoa, farro, brown rice, oats, barley, and whole-grain pasta keep well in sealed containers. Keep a selection on hand so you always have several to choose from.

Canned beans: Keep a variety of chickpeas, black beans, cannellini beans, and kidney beans on hand, and look for reduced-sodium versions when possible.

Canned fish: Tuna, salmon, and sardines have omega-3 fatty acids and are easy to add to salads, sandwiches, and even pasta or eggs. Look for varieties that are packed in water or olive oil.

Coconut milk and almond milk: Both are available in shelf-stable varieties, so they are nice to keep in the pantry. Light coconut milk is great in curries, smoothies, and oatmeal. Almond milk works well in overnight oats and smoothies, too.

Olive oil: Buy a large bottle of extra-virgin olive oil to use for all your cooking. To preserve the oil's flavor, keep it in the pantry, away from direct sunlight and the heat of the stove.

Spices: It's good to have a variety of dried spices that you'll use often, such as kosher salt (which has less sodium than table salt), pepper, onion powder, garlic powder, basil, oregano, cinnamon, and nutmeg.

Onions and garlic: Garlic and red, white, and sweet onions are the base for many meals, so try to always have them on hand.

Refrigerator and Freezer

- **Frozen and fresh fruits and vegetables:** Frozen berries are packed at the peak of ripeness, so they offer the same nutrition as fresh ones! The same is true for frozen vegetables. Buy fresh fruits and vegetables when they are in season and buy frozen when they're not.

- **Green leafy vegetables:** You will be eating these daily, so keep a variety in the refrigerator. Spinach (fresh or frozen), kale, and Swiss chard are a good place to start.

- **Condiments:** Mustard, roasted red peppers, sun-dried tomatoes, curry paste, and tahini add lots of flavor and make great additions to sandwiches and dressings.

- **Frozen seafood:** Buy salmon, shrimp, and cod frozen rather than fresh unless you are going to use it within 48 hours.

- **Chicken and turkey (breasts, thighs, and cutlets):** Keep a variety of cuts in the freezer. They're easy to pull out to make a quick sheet-pan dinner or to grill and toss into a salad in a pinch.

- **Nuts and seeds:** Keep a variety of nuts—almonds, walnuts, pistachios, peanuts, and pecans—and seeds on hand. Look for unsalted nuts and store them in the freezer. They defrost quickly and can be toasted or added to dishes once thawed.

Kitchen Equipment

- **8-inch cast-iron pan and 10-inch nonstick or stainless-steel skillet:** These pans are the perfect size for making two portions of most dishes.

- **6- to 8-quart stockpot or Dutch oven:** This vessel is a must-have for making soups and boiling pasta.

- **Food processor or blender:** You can use either to make smoothies and whip up hummus, dressing, or dip. A handheld blender works well for pureeing soups but is not necessary.

- **Baking sheets:** Baking sheets with a rim are great to have for sheet-pan dinners and baked goods. A couple of 9-by-13-inch or 11-by-16-inch baking sheets are perfect for making two portions.

- **Good-quality knives:** A chef's knife, paring knife, and serrated bread knife are the tools you'll use most often. It pays to invest in good-quality knives and to keep them sharpened. Doing so will save you time and reduce the risk of cutting yourself.

MIND-FUL ACTIVITIES TO DO TOGETHER

Part of keeping your mind young is keeping your brain stimulated. Doing new and fun things with the other half of your duo and challenging yourself are excellent ways to give your brain a workout and strengthen the connections throughout your brain.

- **Learn a new game.** Try your hand at cribbage, Scrabble, or another mind-challenging game. Invite two other people over or set up a neighborhood game night. It's a great way to socialize and have fun, too.

- **Take dance lessons.** In addition to learning something new, you'll work on your coordination skills, spend quality time together, and get some exercise.

- **Get outside!** Explore your neighborhood, take a tour of a local attraction, walk through a local park, or head out to a biking trail you've always wanted to try. You'll get fresh air and exercise, and you'll keep your brain active by learning something new about where you live.

- **Pick up a new hobby.** Whether bird watching, photography, golf, or cooking, find something you can do and learn together and have fun doing it.

- **Cutting boards:** Having two cutting boards is ideal and helps prevent cross-contamination. Use one for fruits and vegetables and one for meat, poultry, and fish.

- **A variety of bowls in different sizes:** You'll want to have glass and stainless-steel bowls in a variety of sizes for mixing ingredients. They are also useful for assembling all your ingredients ahead of time so meal prep goes faster.

- **Handheld citrus juicer:** This appliance is a must! You will use a lot of citrus juice in these recipes because it adds a burst of flavor and reduces the need for salt.

About the Recipes

Although most of the recipes in this book are designed for two people, there are a few that make four portions and are easy to freeze. Feel free to double any of the recipes if you want leftovers.

All the recipes include serving sizes, nutritional information, and helpful labels so you will know exactly what you are eating and can make sure the dish fits into your eating plan.

Recipe Labels

DAIRY-FREE These recipes do not contain any milk, cheese, dairy-based yogurt, or butter.

5-INGREDIENT These recipes use five ingredients or fewer, not including salt, pepper, oil, or butter.

GLUTEN-FREE These recipes do not contain wheat, barley, rye, or oats.

ONE-POT You can make these recipes in one pot or pan, so cleanup is a snap!

QUICK These recipes take 30 minutes or less to prepare.

VEGAN Recipes with this label do not contain any meat, fish, dairy, or eggs.

VEGETARIAN Recipes with this label do not contain any meat.

Recipe Help

Many of the recipes include tips that will help expand your cooking and nutrition knowledge and provide ideas for how to adjust the recipe.

Cooking tip: These tips explain certain cooking techniques or how to make the cooking process or preparation easier.

Use it again: Sometimes it makes sense to prepare extra of an ingredient, and this tip will give you suggestions for other ways you can use it.

Variation tip: These tips provide ideas for how to adjust the recipe to accommodate allergies or ingredient substitutions.

CHAPTER 2

Breakfast and Smoothies

Avocado Green Smoothie

Makes 2 (12-ounce) smoothies **Prep Time:** 10 minutes

Although avocados are high in fat, it's good brain-healthy fat! Avocados also contain vitamin K, potassium, and vitamin C, important nutrients for brain health. This smoothie is a good way to use up extra spinach.

4 cups packed fresh spinach

½ cup coarsely chopped fresh flat-leaf parsley, leaves and stems

1 cup vanilla or plain almond milk, divided

2 medium avocados, pitted, peeled, and diced

2 (5.3-ounce) vanilla-flavored almond yogurt cartons

2 ice cubes

¼ cup lime juice

2 teaspoons honey (optional)

1. In the bowl of a food processor, place the spinach, parsley, and ¼ cup of almond milk and process until almost pureed.

2. Add the avocados, the remaining ¾ cup of almond milk, the yogurt, and ice cubes and process until smooth.

3. While the processor is running slowly, pour the lime juice through the feed tube into the mixture and blend until thoroughly combined. Drizzle in the honey (if using) and blend quickly.

4. Divide between two glasses and enjoy.

COOKING TIP: To save time and reduce food waste, gather the parsley in a bunch and cut off the bottom stems. Reserve them and use to make a pot of Homemade Vegetable Broth (page 109). The small stems that remain attached to the leaves can be blended into the smoothie.

PER SERVING (1 SMOOTHIE): Calories: 485; Total fat: 31g; Saturated fat: 4g; Cholesterol: 0mg; Sodium: 271mg; Carbohydrates: 43g; Fiber: 16g;Sugar: 22g; Protein: 16g

Blueberry Smoothie

Makes 2 (10-ounce) smoothies **Prep Time:** 5 minutes

Antioxidant-rich blueberries are the star of this delicious smoothie. The kefir and yogurt are rich in probiotics that support gut health and the immune system and may help reduce inflammation. You can use any flavor of yogurt (as long as it's low in sugar), but my favorite is lime, which really brightens up and complements the blueberry flavor.

1½ cups kefir

1 (5.3-ounce) Greek yogurt carton

¼ cup finely chopped walnuts

1 cup fresh blueberries

2 or 3 ice cubes

1. In a blender or food processor, place the kefir, yogurt, walnuts, blueberries, and ice cubes. Blend about 1 minute on high, until the mixture is completely combined and blue in color.

2. Divide between two glasses and enjoy.

VARIATION TIP: Frozen blueberries are great to use in a smoothie. You don't need to thaw them; just add them to the mix and puree. You can also replace the kefir with regular milk if you prefer. You may need only 1 or 2 ice cubes if you use milk.

PER SERVING (1 SMOOTHIE): Calories: 261; Total fat: 14g; Saturated fat: 4g; Cholesterol: 17mg; Sodium: 121mg; Carbohydrates: 25g; Fiber: 3g; Sugar: 20g; Protein: 12g

Overnight Oats with Strawberries and Almonds

Serves 2 **Prep Time:** 10 minutes, plus 8 hours to chill

This recipe is one of the easiest make-ahead breakfasts, and it's a regular part of my weekly routine. Oatmeal is an excellent source of fiber, and when combined with nuts and milk, it makes a protein-packed breakfast that will keep you satisfied all morning. The chia seeds add a boost of omega-3 fatty acids, too!

1 cup old-fashioned oats

2 teaspoons brown sugar

2 tablespoons chia seeds

1½ cups almond or
  soy milk

1 cup chopped
  strawberries

¼ cup sliced almonds

1. In a 10- to 12-ounce mason jar or container, combine ½ cup of oats, 1 teaspoon of brown sugar, and 1 tablespoon of chia seeds. In a second container, combine the remaining ½ cup of oats, 1 teaspoon of brown sugar, and 1 tablespoon of chia seeds.

2. Add ¾ cup of milk to each container, stir, seal, and place in the refrigerator to chill overnight.

3. In the morning, remove the jars from the refrigerator. Mix ½ cup of strawberries and 2 tablespoons of almonds into each container of oatmeal and enjoy chilled. Or, to enjoy it warmed, place the contents of the jar in a microwave-safe bowl and heat in the microwave for 30 seconds to 1 minute. Top with the strawberries and almonds and enjoy.

VARIATION TIP: You can make this dish your own by changing up the fruit, nuts, and milk. Try blueberries, blackberries, chopped mango, or cherries instead of strawberries, and use pecans, walnuts, or hazelnuts in place of the almonds. Use regular milk, coconut milk, or oat milk. Add honey in place of the brown sugar, or add no sweetener at all. The options are endless!

PER SERVING: Calories: 335; Total fat: 16g; Saturated fat: 2g; Cholesterol: 0mg; Sodium: 95mg; Carbohydrates: 47g; Fiber: 14g; Sugar: 14g; Protein: 16g

Apricot-Almond Breakfast Bars

Makes 4 (2-inch-by-2-inch) bars **Prep Time:** 10 minutes, plus 3 to 8 hours to chill

Almonds and almond butter are a great source of heart- and brain-healthy monounsaturated fat and are full of protein, magnesium, vitamin E, and calcium. These little bars are a sweet treat that will keep you energized all morning long.

½ cup dried apricots

¼ cup almond butter

¼ cup old-fashioned oats

2 tablespoons maple syrup

¼ teaspoon cinnamon

½ cup sliced almonds, divided

COOKING TIP: Try toasting the sliced almonds. Toasting brings the oils to the surface, pulling out more of that delicious nutty flavor.

1. In the bowl of a food processor, place the apricots, almond butter, oats, maple syrup, cinnamon, and ¼ cup of sliced almonds. Puree for 20 to 30 seconds, until all the ingredients are well combined and the mixture pulls away from the side of the processor.

2. On a piece of parchment paper, spread the mixture into a 4-inch-by-4-inch square. Sprinkle the remaining ¼ cup of sliced almonds over the top and press into the mixture, making it an even thickness. Wrap the parchment paper tightly around the square.

3. Place the square in the freezer for 3 to 4 hours, or overnight. Remove the oatmeal mixture from the freezer and let it thaw slightly, 5 to 10 minutes, then cut it into 4 squares.

4. This recipe makes enough for two breakfasts or snacks. Wrap the remaining 2 bars in parchment paper, place them in a resealable plastic bag, and store in the refrigerator for up to 1 week or in the freezer for up to 1 month.

PER SERVING (1 BAR): Calories: 252; Total fat: 15g; Saturated fat: 2g; Cholesterol: 0mg; Sodium: 39mg; Carbohydrates: 26g; Fiber: 5g; Sugar: 16g; Protein: 7g

Triple-Berry Mini Dutch Baby

Makes 1 medium-size Dutch baby **Prep Time:** 10 minutes **Cook Time:** 30 minutes

This classic Dutch baby (German pancake) is baked in the oven, and the sides puff up, making it a perfect vessel for the berries. It's a decadent treat for a relaxing weekend morning.

2 eggs

¾ cup nonfat milk

2 tablespoons melted butter, divided

½ teaspoon almond extract

½ cup all-purpose flour

1 tablespoon sugar

1 cup fresh berries (blueberries, strawberries, and blackberries)

Powdered sugar, for garnish

Sliced almonds, for garnish (optional)

1. Preheat the oven to 400°F. Place an 8-inch cast-iron pan in the oven to warm.

2. In a small bowl, whisk together the eggs, milk, 1 tablespoon of butter, and the almond extract. Slowly whisk in the flour and sugar.

3. Using an oven mitt, carefully remove the heated pan from the oven. Put the remaining 1 tablespoon of butter in the skillet, turning to coat the bottom and sides. Pour the batter into the hot pan and place the pan back in the oven.

4. Bake for 25 to 30 minutes, or until the sides have puffed up and the center is flat. Remove the Dutch baby from the oven and place the berries in the center. Dust with powdered sugar and sprinkle with almonds. Divide it in half and serve.

COOKING TIP: Although the MIND diet limits the use of butter to 1 tablespoon a week, I do use butter in this dish for the flavor and browning that is needed. Remember, a little is okay!

PER SERVING (½ OF AN 8-INCH DUTCH BABY): Calories: 386; Total fat: 17g; Saturated fat: 9g; Cholesterol: 218mg; Sodium: 212mg; Carbohydrates: 46g; Fiber: 3g; Sugar: 18g; Protein: 13g

Buckwheat Pancakes with Cinnamon Apples

Makes 6 pancakes **Prep Time:** 15 minutes **Cook Time:** 5 minutes

Buckwheat isn't actually wheat; it's gluten-free whole grain. Buckwheat is a good source of fiber, as well as B vitamins, potassium, and magnesium, which are important for maintaining blood flow to the brain and controlling blood pressure.

¼ cup pumpkin puree

½ cup soy milk

½ cup buckwheat flour

¼ cup gluten-free all-purpose flour

2 tablespoons dark brown sugar

1 teaspoon baking powder

¼ teaspoon kosher salt

3 tablespoons aquafaba (see tip)

1 tablespoon granulated sugar

Nonstick cooking spray

1 medium apple, diced

2 tablespoons chopped walnuts

¼ teaspoon cinnamon

Maple syrup (optional)

COOKING TIP: Aquafaba, the liquid from a can of chickpeas, makes a great egg substitute. It whips up just like egg whites.

1. In a small bowl, whisk together the pumpkin puree and soy milk. Set aside.

2. In a medium bowl, combine the buckwheat flour, all-purpose flour, brown sugar, baking powder, and salt. Set aside.

3. In another small bowl, whip the aquafaba for 5 to 10 minutes, until thick and soft peaks form. Slowly whip in the granulated sugar.

4. Heat a nonstick griddle or large skillet over medium heat and coat it with cooking spray.

5. Add the pumpkin-milk mixture to the flour mixture and stir until combined. Gently fold the aquafaba into the mixture to combine.

6. Using about 3 tablespoons of batter per pancake, spoon out 6 pancakes onto the hot griddle. Press down slightly to form rounds. Cook for about 2 minutes per side, or until browned. Divide between two plates.

7. In a small bowl, toss the apple and walnuts with cinnamon. Place half the mixture on top of each stack of pancakes. Top with maple syrup (if using).

PER SERVING (3 PANCAKES): Calories: 123; Total fat: 2g; Saturated fat: 0g; Cholesterol: 0mg; Sodium: 111mg; Carbohydrates: 24g; Fiber: 3g; Sugar: 11g; Protein: 3g

Mini Egg Frittatas with Spinach

Makes 4 frittatas **Prep Time:** 10 minutes **Cook Time:** 20 minutes

Most frittatas include cheese, but you won't miss it in these flavorful little muffin-shaped frittatas. Enjoy them with an English muffin or a hearty piece of grain toast.

Nonstick cooking spray

2 large eggs, beaten

2 tablespoons low-fat milk

¼ cup chopped fresh spinach

1 tablespoon chopped fresh basil

⅛ teaspoon freshly ground black pepper

⅛ teaspoon kosher salt (optional)

1 tablespoon chopped jarred roasted red peppers

1. Preheat the oven to 350°F. Spray 4 cups of a muffin tin with the cooking spray.

2. In a glass measuring cup or a medium bowl, whisk together the eggs and milk. Stir in the spinach, basil, black pepper, and salt (if using).

3. Divide the mixture evenly among the prepared muffin tin cups. Top each cup with a few pieces of the red pepper.

4. Place the muffin tin in the center of the oven and bake for 15 to 18 minutes, or until the frittatas are puffed on the sides and firm to the touch.

5. Remove and enjoy hot.

USE IT AGAIN: You can easily double this recipe and freeze the extra frittatas for another day. Remove the frittatas from the muffin tin, allow them to cool, then wrap them tightly in plastic wrap and freeze for up to 3 months.

PER SERVING (2 FRITTATAS): Calories: 83; Total fat: 5g; Saturated fat: 2g; Cholesterol: 187mg; Sodium: 81mg; Carbohydrates: 2g; Fiber: 0g; Sugar: 1g; Protein: 7g

Shakshuka

Serves 2 **Prep Time:** 15 minutes **Cook Time:** 20 minutes

Shakshuka is a North African tomato-based dish with poached eggs. (It's also popular in Middle Eastern cooking.) I like to add a healthy dose of carotenoid-rich leafy greens to this recipe. The greens and the choline from the eggs are an excellent combination for brain health.

1 teaspoon extra-virgin olive oil

½ cup sliced sweet onion

½ cup cubed eggplant

2 teaspoons minced garlic

½ cup sliced red, yellow, or orange bell pepper

1 (14.5-ounce) can fire-roasted tomatoes with chiles, undrained

1 cup chopped Swiss chard leaves

1 cup chopped curly kale

2 eggs

1. In a medium skillet or cast-iron pan, heat the olive oil over medium heat. Add the onion and eggplant and cook for about 5 minutes, turning periodically to brown the eggplant and caramelize the onion.

2. Add the garlic and bell pepper and reduce the heat to medium-low. Sauté for about 2 minutes, until the pepper starts to soften, being careful not to burn the garlic.

3. Add the tomatoes with their juices and cook until just bubbling. Then mix in the Swiss chard and kale and cook for about 2 minutes, until the greens are wilted.

4. Make 2 deep wells in the mixture, then gently crack 1 egg into each well. Cover the skillet and cook on low heat until the eggs are done, 6 to 8 minutes, depending on how firm you like the yolk. Serve with a piece of crusty whole-grain bread.

VARIATION TIP: You can add almost any vegetable to this dish, making it a great way to clean out the refrigerator. Fire-roasted tomatoes with chiles add a nice flavor to this recipe.

PER SERVING: Calories: 151; Total fat: 7g; Saturated fat: 2g; Cholesterol: 164mg; Sodium: 983mg; Carbohydrates: 16g; Fiber: 2g; Sugar: 3g; Protein: 9g

Salmon Breakfast Sandwich

Serves 2 **Prep Time:** 10 minutes **Cook Time:** 5 minutes

Seafood for breakfast? Yes, please! This breakfast sandwich is MIND diet friendly and full of protein, omega-3 fatty acids, hearty grains, and leafy greens, giving you—and your brain—a healthy energy boost.

2 whole-grain English muffins

3 tablespoons Spicy Avocado Dressing (page 108), divided

½ cup fresh baby spinach leaves

1 Roma tomato, thinly sliced

1 (5-ounce) can boneless, skinless salmon, drained

¼ cup microgreens (optional)

1. Split the English muffins in half and toast them. Spread one half of the inside of each toasted muffin with 1 tablespoon of the avocado dressing.

2. Place ¼ cup of the spinach leaves on top of the dressing on each of two muffin halves. Add tomato slices on top of the spinach.

3. In a small bowl, gently toss the salmon with the remaining 1 tablespoon of avocado dressing. Be careful not to break up the salmon too much.

4. Place the salmon on top of the tomatoes on each muffin. Add the microgreens (if using), then place the other half of the English muffin on top to form a sandwich. Serve.

USE IT AGAIN: If you have salmon left over from another meal, you can use it in place of the canned salmon. And if you have arugula left over from another meal, try that in place of the spinach to add a peppery note to this sandwich.

PER SERVING (1 SANDWICH): Calories: 242; Total fat: 6g; Saturated fat: 1g; Cholesterol: 47mg; Sodium: 465mg; Carbohydrates: 29g; Fiber: 6g; Sugar: 6g; Protein: 20g

CHAPTER 3
Soups, Salads, and Sandwiches

Lentil Stew with Swiss Chard

Serves 4 **Prep Time:** 15 minutes **Cook Time:** 45 minutes

This hearty stew reminds me of my honeymoon in Italy. Sitting in the kitchen of a 700-year-old farmhouse, my husband and I had small bowls of an amazing lentil soup along with crostini drizzled with olive oil from the farm. Although you may not be eating it in Italy, this soup still evokes cozy Mediterranean vibes. Freeze the extra portions for another dinner down the road.

1 tablespoon extra-virgin olive oil

½ cup chopped yellow onion

½ cup sliced carrots

8 ounces cremini mushrooms, sliced

½ teaspoon dried thyme

½ teaspoon freshly ground black pepper

1 cup (8 ounces) dried brown lentils

4 cups Homemade Vegetable Broth (page 109)

1 (14.5-ounce) can diced tomatoes, undrained

2 cups sliced Swiss chard leaves

Kosher salt (optional)

1. In a large stockpot, heat the olive oil over medium-low heat. Add the onion and carrots and sauté for 2 to 3 minutes, until just beginning to soften. Add the mushrooms, thyme, and pepper and continue cooking for another 5 minutes, until soft.

2. Stir in the lentils and toss with the vegetables to coat them with olive oil. Add the broth and bring the mixture to a boil. Reduce the heat to low, cover, and cook for 30 minutes, or until the lentils are softened. Add the tomatoes with their juices and cook for another 1 to 2 minutes.

3. Transfer half the mixture to the bowl of a food processor and pulse to puree the lentils and vegetables. Return the puree to the pot and mix. There will be some creaminess in the mixture with some whole vegetables remaining.

4. Add the Swiss chard to the pot and heat to wilt the chard, 2 to 3 minutes. Season with salt and pepper if needed. Serve with crusty bread and a salad.

PER SERVING (1½ CUPS): Calories: 246; Total fat: 4g; Saturated fat: 1g; Cholesterol: 0mg; Sodium: 181mg; Carbohydrates: 41g; Fiber: 9g; Sugar: 6g; Protein: 15g

Butternut Squash Soup with Kale

Serves 4 **Prep Time:** 10 minutes **Cook Time:** 45 minutes

This savory butternut squash soup is a fall staple in my house. I like adding an apple with a bit of a bite to this recipe to help balance out the sweetness of the squash, so I usually go with Granny Smith, but Honeycrisp works well, too.

1 tablespoon extra-virgin olive oil

1 cup chopped Spanish or yellow onion

4 cups cubed butternut squash

1 Granny Smith apple, peeled, cored, and chopped

½ cup apple cider

4 cups Homemade Vegetable Broth (page 109)

2 cups chopped curly kale

Kosher salt (optional)

1. In a large stockpot, heat the olive oil over medium-low heat. Add the onion and cook for 3 to 4 minutes, until just softened. Add the butternut squash and apple and cook for 2 minutes more.

2. Stir in the apple cider and bring the soup to a low boil. Cook for 5 minutes, allowing the cider to thicken. Add the broth and bring the soup to a boil. Reduce the heat to low, cover, and simmer for 30 minutes.

3. Once the squash and apples are softened, using an immersion blender, puree the soup in the pot. Alternatively, place 2 cups at a time in a food processor or blender and carefully process until smooth, then pour the soup back into the pot.

4. Add the kale to the soup. Simmer for 2 to 3 minutes, or until the kale is wilted. Season with salt if desired. Serve with crusty multigrain bread and a salad.

COOKING TIP: This makes four servings so you can have leftovers for another night or freeze the rest for later. Store in the refrigerator for 3 days or in the freezer for 3 months.

PER SERVING (1½ CUPS): Calories: 143; Total fat: 4g; Saturated fat: 1g; Cholesterol: 0mg; Sodium: 12mg; Carbohydrates: 27g; Fiber: 5g; Sugar: 9g; Protein: 2g

Tuscan Bean Soup

Serves 4 **Prep Time:** 5 minutes **Cook Time:** 30 minutes

Cannellini beans are a classic part of Tuscan cuisine. They're high in fiber and protein, making them a smart addition to soups and casseroles to help you easily get the recommended three servings of beans per week.

1 tablespoon extra-virgin olive oil

½ cup chopped sweet onion

1 (11-ounce) package of Italian-style chicken sausage

1 (14.5-ounce) can diced tomatoes, undrained

1 (15.5-ounce) can cannellini beans, drained and rinsed

4 cups reduced-sodium chicken broth

2 tablespoons Pesto Sauce (page 106)

1 cup small pasta, such as ditalini

6 cups fresh baby spinach

1. In a large stockpot, heat the olive oil over medium-low heat. Add the onion and cook for about 3 minutes, until just softened.

2. Slice the sausage into ½-inch-thick rounds. Add the sausage to the pot and cook for 3 minutes.

3. Stir in the tomatoes with their juices, the beans, and broth and cook for 10 minutes.

4. Add the pesto sauce and pasta, increase the heat to medium-high, and bring to a low boil. Cook for about 10 minutes, until the pasta is al dente. Stir in the spinach, allowing it to wilt and cook down, about 1 minute.

5. Serve hot. Save the remaining two portions for another meal or freeze for up to 3 months.

VARIATION TIP: Swap the chicken sausage for a hot Italian sausage, or for a vegetarian version, skip the sausage altogether.

PER SERVING (1½ CUPS): Calories: 417; Total fat: 15g; Saturated fat: 2g; Cholesterol: 60mg; Sodium: 491mg; Carbohydrates: 44g; Fiber: 10g; Sugar: 5g; Protein: 27g

Tomato Soup

Serves 4 **Prep Time:** 5 minutes, plus 15 minutes to cool **Cook Time:** 25 minutes

This thick and rich tomato soup is full of the antioxidant lycopene, which has been shown to help reduce inflammation and may help reduce LDL cholesterol, which can lead to plaque buildup in the arteries. Research has shown that our bodies absorb more lycopene from tomatoes that have been heated.

1 tablespoon extra-virgin olive oil, plus more for drizzling

½ cup chopped sweet onion

1 (6-ounce) can tomato paste with roasted garlic

1 (28-ounce) can whole tomatoes

2 cups Homemade Vegetable Broth (page 109)

1 teaspoon sugar

¼ teaspoon kosher salt

½ teaspoon freshly ground black pepper

Chopped fresh basil, for garnish

1. In a large stockpot or Dutch oven, heat the olive oil over medium heat. Add the onion and cook for 3 to 4 minutes, until just softened.

2. Add the tomato paste and mix into the onion and cook for 1 minute. Add the tomatoes, broth, sugar, salt, and pepper. Slowly heat to a low boil, then reduce the heat to low and simmer for 15 minutes.

3. Cool the soup for 10 to 15 minutes, then blend in the pot with an immersion blender. Alternatively, after cooling, transfer the soup to a food processor or blender, and puree in two or three batches.

4. Serve with fresh basil and a drizzle of olive oil.

VARIATION TIP: If you can't find tomato paste with roasted garlic, use 1 can of tomato paste and 1 teaspoon of minced garlic instead.

PER SERVING (1¼ CUPS): Calories: 109; Total fat: 4g; Saturated fat: 1g; Cholesterol: 0mg; Sodium: 453mg; Carbohydrates: 18g; Fiber: 6g; Sugar: 11g; Protein: 3g

Mediterranean Tuna and White Bean Salad

Serves 2 **Prep Time:** 10 minutes

Tuna salad usually conjures visions of tiny pieces of tuna smothered in mayonnaise with some celery and relish, but not this version. The tuna in olive oil, combined with a little pesto and lots of vegetables and beans, is so satisfying that you'll never think of tuna salad the same way.

1 (4.5-ounce) can yellowfin or albacore tuna in olive oil

½ cup diced red and yellow bell pepper

2 tablespoons diced sweet onion

½ cup diced artichoke hearts

1 cup cannellini beans, drained and rinsed

2 tablespoons Pesto Sauce (page 106)

4 cups spring mix

1. Place the tuna along with the oil from the can in a medium bowl. Break the fish into chunks with a fork. Mix in the bell pepper, onion, artichoke hearts, and beans. Add the pesto sauce and mix gently to combine.

2. Divide the spring mix between two plates and top each evenly with the tuna mixture. Serve with a piece of crusty whole-grain bread on the side to sop up any leftover sauce.

VARIATION TIP: There are different kinds of tuna available in most grocery stores, so if you aren't familiar with them, it can be confusing. Yellowfin tuna is a bit more tender and flavorful, whereas albacore tuna is firmer and a little blander. Either variety works well in this dish, but make sure it is packed in olive oil, not water.

PER SERVING: Calories: 360; Total fat: 14g; Saturated fat: 2g; Cholesterol: 19mg; Sodium: 387mg; Carbohydrates: 34g; Fiber: 15g; Sugar: 3g; Protein: 26g

Kale, Chard, and Delicata Squash Salad

Serves 2 **Prep Time:** 15 minutes **Cook Time:** 20 minutes

Delicata squash is a small squash with a tender edible skin. The sweetness of the squash helps balance the bitterness of the kale and chard, and the oil from the dressing helps you absorb the antioxidants from the squash and leafy greens.

FOR THE DRESSING

2 tablespoons extra-virgin olive oil

1 tablespoon white wine vinegar

2 teaspoons maple syrup

2 teaspoons Dijon mustard

1 teaspoon finely chopped shallots

Freshly ground black pepper

FOR THE SALAD

1 small delicata squash

¼ red onion, cut into 1-inch slices

1 teaspoon extra-virgin olive oil

1 cup chopped Tuscan kale

1 cup chopped Swiss chard leaves

2 tablespoons chopped dates

2 tablespoons chopped pecans

TO MAKE THE DRESSING

1. In a small bowl, place the olive oil, vinegar, maple syrup, mustard, and shallots. Whisk until combined. Season with pepper to taste. Set aside.

TO MAKE THE SALAD

2. Preheat the oven to 425°F.

3. Cut the squash in half lengthwise and remove the seeds. Cut the squash into ½-inch slices and place the slices in a medium bowl. Add the onion, toss with the olive oil, and spread the vegetables out on a baking sheet. Roast for 20 minutes, until the squash is tender and the edges are browned. Allow the vegetables to cool.

4. In a medium bowl, place the kale and chard. Add half the dressing and toss the greens well to coat thoroughly. Add the dates and pecans and top with the squash. Divide between two plates and serve with the remaining dressing on the side.

VARIATION TIP: Chopped pistachios or walnuts would also be delicious in place of the pecans.

PER SERVING: Calories: 333; Total fat: 21g; Saturated fat: 3g; Cholesterol: 0mg; Sodium: 106mg; Carbohydrates: 38g; Fiber: 6g; Sugar: 11g; Protein: 4g

Orange Quinoa-Chickpea Salad

Serves 2 **Prep Time:** 15 minutes

Quinoa is considered a complete protein, meaning it has all the essential amino acids our bodies need for growth and development. Quinoa is also rich in fiber and a variety of minerals and B vitamins that are essential for brain health.

FOR THE DRESSING

2 tablespoons orange juice (squeezed from the sectioned orange)

2 tablespoons extra-virgin olive oil

½ teaspoon honey

¼ teaspoon kosher salt

¼ teaspoon freshly ground black pepper

FOR THE SALAD

1 cup cooked quinoa

1 orange, zested, peeled, and sectioned

¼ cup finely chopped red onion

½ cup canned chickpeas, drained and rinsed

½ cup finely chopped baby spinach

2 tablespoons chopped toasted walnuts

2 teaspoons chopped fresh basil

TO MAKE THE DRESSING

1. In a small bowl, whisk together the orange juice, olive oil, honey, salt, and pepper until emulsified. Set aside.

TO MAKE THE SALAD

2. In a medium bowl, combine the quinoa, orange zest and segments, onion, chickpeas, and spinach. Add the walnuts and basil and combine well.

3. Pour the dressing over the salad and toss together to coat all the ingredients. Store the salad in the refrigerator to allow the flavors to soak in and blend together before serving. The salad can be stored in the refrigerator for up to 2 days.

COOKING TIP: To section the orange, slice off the top and bottom of the fruit, cutting as close to the fruit as possible. Then stand the orange on one end and make vertical cuts all around the peel, cutting as closely to the fruit as possible to remove the peel. Once peeled, gently cut along the sections, or membranes, toward the center of the orange. The citrus sections will fall out, leaving just the thin paper-like separations attached to the center. Squeeze the membranes that are left into a small bowl to get any remaining juice.

PER SERVING: Calories: 403; Total fat: 21g; Saturated fat: 3g; Cholesterol: 0mg; Sodium: 173mg; Carbohydrates: 46g; Fiber: 8g; Sugar: 13g; Protein: 10g

Pan Bagnat with Tuna

Serves 2 **Prep Time:** 10 minutes

I haven't been fortunate enough to visit France yet, but I know a pan bagnat will be high on my list to try as soon as I get there. What could be better than a tuna niçoise salad stuffed in a baguette? Typically, these sandwiches include olives and capers, which add a nice bite but are high in salt. I've replaced them with a little red wine vinegar to give the sandwich its classic bite while keeping the sodium content down.

2 (6-inch) baguettes

1 cup fresh baby spinach

⅛ cup red onion slices, soaked in water (see tip)

¼ cup roasted red pepper strips

1 hard-boiled egg

1 (4.5-ounce) can yellowfin tuna in olive oil

⅛ cup sliced basil leaves

½ teaspoon red wine vinegar

1. Cut the baguettes in half lengthwise.

2. Lay ½ cup of spinach over the bottom of one baguette half and repeat with the other baguette half. Top each with half the red onion and half the roasted red pepper strips.

3. Cut the hard-boiled egg into 4 slices and lay 2 slices over the vegetables on each sandwich. Break the tuna into chunks, then top each sandwich with half the tuna. Sprinkle each sandwich with half the basil leaves and drizzle with ¼ teaspoon of red wine vinegar and some of the olive oil from the tuna.

COOKING TIP: Soaking the red onion slices in cool water for 10 to 15 minutes cuts down on the bite and brings out the sweet flavor of the onion.

PER SERVING: Calories: 363; Total fat: 9g; Saturated fat: 2g; Cholesterol: 103mg; Sodium: 525mg; Carbohydrates: 45g; Fiber: 3g; Sugar: 1g; Protein: 26g

Open-Faced Sun-Dried Tomato Sandwich

Serves 2 **Prep Time:** 10 minutes **Cook Time:** 5 minutes

I love this zesty open-faced sandwich on a cool spring day or with a cup of soup in the winter. The arugula lends a peppery bite, and it is an easy way to get in a serving of greens. The walnuts are a plant-based source of omega-3s, and the cannellini beans add protein and fiber, making this a hearty and satisfying lunch or casual dinner. This sandwich is delicious with Tomato Soup (page 35).

1 cup cannellini beans, drained and rinsed

¼ cup oil-packed sun-dried tomatoes plus 1 tablespoon oil

4 slices whole-grain bread

2 ounces walnuts, chopped (about 2 tablespoons)

½ cup baby arugula

1. In the bowl of a food processor, place the beans, sun-dried tomatoes, and the oil from the tomato jar. Process until pureed and smooth.

2. Toast the bread.

3. Spread a quarter of the bean and tomato mixture on each slice of bread. Top each slice with ½ tablespoon of walnuts and a quarter of the arugula.

USE IT AGAIN: Double the bean and tomato mixture and use it as a dip for vegetables, pita chips, or crackers, or spread it on toast and top with a poached egg for a hearty breakfast.

PER SERVING: Calories: 481; Total fat: 23g; Saturated fat: 3g; Cholesterol: 0mg; Sodium: 237mg; Carbohydrates: 53g; Fiber: 16g; Sugar: 5g; Protein: 20g

Hummus and Vegetable Wrap

Serves 2 **Prep Time:** 10 minutes

This wrap is just like a deli sandwich, but I made it MIND diet friendly by filling it with leafy greens, legumes, and vegetables. The baby arugula, hummus, and tahini dressing are delicious combined with lots of veggies on a seasoned wrap. These can be made in the morning, wrapped tightly in plastic wrap, and kept in the refrigerator or packed in a cooler to go. They make a perfect lunch after a hike or bike ride in the park.

2 (8-inch) sun-dried tomato or spinach wraps

¼ cup Hummus (page 94)

¼ red bell pepper, cut into thin strips

¼ yellow bell pepper, cut into thin strips

2 tablespoons red onion slices

¼ cup thinly sliced cucumbers

1 cup baby arugula

2 teaspoons Tahini Dressing (page 107)

1. Place a sandwich wrap on a plate. Spread 2 tablespoons of hummus down the center of the wrap, leaving a 1-inch border on each end.

2. Place half the red and yellow bell peppers, red onion, and cucumbers on top of the hummus, top with ½ cup of arugula, and drizzle with 1 teaspoon of dressing.

3. Fold up the opposite ends of the wrap a quarter of the way over the filling, and then pull one of the sides over the vegetables and wrap it tightly. Slice in half. Repeat steps 1 through 3 with the second wrap and serve.

VARIATION TIP: Add sliced turkey or tuna for a non-vegetarian version, and substitute baby spinach for the arugula if desired.

PER SERVING (1 WRAP): Calories: 219; Total fat: 6g; Saturated fat: 1g; Cholesterol: 0mg; Sodium: 426mg; Carbohydrates: 36g; Fiber: 3g; Sugar: 3g; Protein: 6g

CHAPTER 4
Plant-Based Mains

Chickpea Curry with Bok Choy

Serves 2 **Prep Time:** 15 minutes **Cook Time:** 15 minutes

Bok choy is a leafy green cruciferous vegetable that's rich in brain-healthy vitamin K, potassium, and antioxidants. It makes a nice addition to stir-fries, curries, and salads.

2 teaspoons extra-virgin olive oil

½ cup thinly sliced sweet onion

½ cup sliced red bell pepper

1 teaspoon minced garlic

½ tablespoon red curry paste

½ cup light coconut milk

½ cup Homemade Vegetable Broth (page 109)

1 teaspoon lime zest

2 teaspoons lime juice

1 cup canned chickpeas, drained and rinsed

2 cups thinly sliced bok choy

2 cups cooked brown rice

1. In a large skillet, heat the olive oil over medium heat. Add the onion and bell pepper and sauté for 3 to 4 minutes, until just starting to soften. Add the garlic and cook for 1 minute more, stirring to prevent it from browning.

2. Add the red curry paste and cook for 1 minute. Slowly add the coconut milk and stir until it combines with the curry paste and turns red. Add the broth, lime zest, lime juice, and chickpeas. Stir to combine and cook for 5 minutes, until the sauce is slightly reduced.

3. Add the bok choy and cook for 1 minute, stirring until wilted.

4. Serve over the brown rice.

USE IT AGAIN: Reserve the chickpea liquid (aquafaba) to use as an egg substitute. Any extra chickpeas can be used to make hummus.

PER SERVING: Calories: 509; Total fat: 16g; Saturated fat: 5g; Cholesterol: 0mg; Sodium: 31mg; Carbohydrates: 80g; Fiber: 14g; Sugar: 10g; Protein: 15g

Farro and Grilled Fruit Bowl

Serves 2 **Prep Time:** 15 minutes

Farro is an ancient grain that has a delicious nutty flavor and is full of fiber and B vitamins. Cook up a batch over the weekend and use it in your meals all week. This sweet and spicy bowl makes a nice hearty lunch for two and can easily be doubled or tripled for a larger group. It is fun to set out bowls with a variety of fruits and vegetables and let everyone create their own.

2 cups fresh baby spinach, shredded

1 cup cooked farro

½ cup (½-inch) diced red bell pepper

½ cup (1-inch) diced grilled pineapple

½ cup (1-inch) diced grilled mango

¼ cup thinly sliced red onion

1 cup canned chickpeas, drained and rinsed

2 tablespoons pumpkin seeds

3 tablespoons Spicy Avocado Dressing (page 108)

1. Line two bowls with 1 cup of spinach each. Top the spinach in each bowl with ½ cup of farro. Place the bell pepper, pineapple, mango, onion, and chickpeas on top of the farro.

2. Sprinkle 1 tablespoon of pumpkin seeds over each bowl and drizzle with 1½ tablespoons of the avocado dressing.

VARIATION TIP: If you follow a gluten-free diet, swap the farro with quinoa, brown rice, or a brown rice and wild rice blend.

PER SERVING (2 CUPS): Calories: 393; Total fat: 9g; Saturated fat: 1g; Cholesterol: 0mg; Sodium: 57mg; Carbohydrates: 67g; Fiber: 14g; Sugar: 19g; Protein: 17g

Eggplant with Tahini Dressing

Serves 2 **Prep Time:** 20 minutes **Cook Time:** 55 minutes

Many recipes that use eggplant tell you to salt it on both sides and let it sit for an hour or more to extract water to improve browning and reduce the bitter flavor, but that is not necessary. Make sure the oil is very hot before you add the eggplant to the pan, and you'll have beautifully browned eggplant that is delicious and tender! I love the meatiness the eggplant and mushrooms add to the dish, and the lemon in the tahini dressing adds a zestiness that pulls all the flavors together.

FOR THE LENTILS AND BROWN RICE

1 teaspoon extra-virgin olive oil

¼ cup finely chopped celery

¼ cup finely chopped onion

¼ cup (¼-inch) diced carrots

2 cups Homemade Vegetable Broth (page 109)

½ cup dried brown lentils

½ cup brown rice ▶

TO MAKE THE LENTILS AND BROWN RICE

1. In a small saucepan, heat the olive oil over medium heat. Stir in the celery, onion, and carrots and cook for 3 minutes, until the onion and celery have softened slightly.

2. Add the broth and bring to a boil. Add the lentils, reduce the heat to low, and simmer for 30 minutes.

3. After the lentils have cooked for 30 minutes, add the rice to the pan, cover, and cook for 20 minutes more, or until all the broth is absorbed.

TO MAKE THE EGGPLANT

4. In a large skillet, heat the grapeseed oil over medium-high heat. When the oil is hot and sizzling, add the eggplant. Cook, stirring, for about 5 minutes, until browned on all sides.

FOR THE EGGPLANT

1 tablespoon grapeseed oil

2 cups (1-inch) diced eggplant

1 cup sliced cremini mushrooms

¼ cup finely chopped sweet onion

1 cup diced tomatoes

½ cup Homemade Vegetable Broth (page 109)

1 teaspoon fresh thyme, or ½ teaspoon dried thyme

1 cup chopped Swiss chard leaves

¼ cup Tahini Dressing (page 107)

5. Add the mushrooms and onion and cook for 2 minutes, stirring to prevent the onion from burning. Add the tomatoes, broth, and thyme and cook for 5 minutes, or until most of the liquid is absorbed. During the last minute, stir in the Swiss chard.

6. Serve 1 cup of the eggplant mixture over 1 cup of the lentil and brown rice mixture and drizzle with the tahini dressing.

USE IT AGAIN: You can make the lentils and rice ahead of time and store it in the refrigerator for up to 3 days, then reheat it in the microwave. Double the lentils and rice if you want to use it later in the week for the Stuffed Flounder with Grain Salad recipe (page 73) or as part of a rice bowl for lunch.

PER SERVING: Calories: 538; Total fat: 15g; Saturated fat: 2g; Cholesterol: 0mg; Sodium: 84mg; Carbohydrates: 84g; Fiber: 13g; Sugar: 10g; Protein: 20g

Balsamic-Glazed Mushroom and Swiss Chard Tart

Makes 2 (6-inch) tarts **Prep Time:** 20 minutes **Cook Time:** 35 minutes

Similar recipes are made with heavy cream and eggs, but this vegan tart uses tofu, which is a great source of protein and isoflavones, a type of antioxidant that has anti-inflammatory properties.

FOR THE CRUST

1 cup all-purpose flour

2 tablespoons extra-virgin olive oil

2 tablespoons ice-cold water

FOR THE TARTS

1 teaspoon extra-virgin olive oil

¼ cup thinly sliced red onion

1 cup thinly sliced cremini mushrooms

¼ teaspoon dried thyme

⅛ teaspoon garlic powder

⅛ teaspoon freshly ground black pepper

1 cup chopped Swiss chard leaves ▶

TO MAKE THE CRUST

1. Pour the flour into a medium bowl. With a fork, mix in the olive oil. Slowly add the water, mixing until just combined, being careful not to overmix. It's okay if the dough is a little crumbly.

2. Gather the dough into a ball and flatten it into a disk. Wrap the disk tightly with plastic wrap and place it in the refrigerator while you prepare the tart ingredients.

TO MAKE THE TARTS

3. Preheat the oven to 375°F.

4. In a medium skillet, heat the olive oil over medium heat. Add the onion and cook for 2 minutes, until just slightly soft. Stir in the mushrooms and cook for 3 to 5 minutes, until browned and dry.

5. Stir in the thyme, garlic powder, and pepper. Add the Swiss chard and cook for 1 to 2 minutes, until wilted. Stir in the dates and set aside.

2 tablespoons chopped
dates

7 ounces firm tofu,
pressed for 20 minutes

1 tablespoon soy-milk
yogurt

⅛ teaspoon nutmeg
(optional)

1 tablespoon balsamic
glaze

6. In the bowl of a food processor, place the tofu, yogurt, and nutmeg (if using). Process quickly to combine. The mixture should be slightly crumbly and soft. Transfer the tofu mixture to a large bowl. Stir in the vegetable mixture and combine well.

7. Place 2 (6-inch) tart pans with removable bottoms on a small baking sheet.

8. To make the tart shells, remove the crust dough from the refrigerator, divide it in half, and form into 2 disks. Roll a disk between 2 pieces of wax paper into a 7-inch circle. Remove the top piece of the wax paper, flip the crust over the tart pan, and remove the bottom piece of wax paper. Using your fingers, press the dough into the pan, making sure it goes completely up the sides of the pan to the top edge. Repeat with the remaining disk.

9. Fill each tart shell with half the tofu and vegetable mixture and smooth out the top. Place the baking sheet with the tarts in the oven. Bake for 20 to 25 minutes, until the filling is firm to the touch and slightly brown.

10. Allow the tarts to cool slightly, then brush with the balsamic glaze and serve.

PER SERVING (1 TART): Calories: 561; Total fat: 25g; Saturated fat: 4g; Cholesterol: 0mg; Sodium: 59mg; Carbohydrates: 64g; Fiber: 6g; Sugar: 9g; Protein: 24g

Chickpea Pasta Primavera

Serves 2 **Prep Time:** 10 minutes **Cook Time:** 20 minutes

Pasta primavera is an easy way to clean out the refrigerator! Although this recipe calls for specific vegetables, feel free to use any veggies you have on hand. Loaded with vegetables and combined with the chickpea pasta, this easy dinner is MIND diet friendly and can be pulled together quickly on a busy weeknight.

2 teaspoons extra-virgin olive oil

¼ cup chopped sweet onion

1 cup diced red, yellow, or orange bell pepper

1 cup diced zucchini

1 cup (1-inch) asparagus pieces

1 cup Zesty Tomato Sauce (page 110)

¼ teaspoon dried oregano

½ teaspoon dried basil

¼ teaspoon freshly ground black pepper

1 cup baby kale

1 cup fresh baby spinach

4 ounces chickpea pasta

1. In a large skillet, heat the olive oil over medium heat. When hot, add the onion and sauté for 2 to 3 minutes, until just softened. Add the bell pepper, zucchini, and asparagus and sauté for 8 minutes. Stir in the tomato sauce, oregano, basil, and black pepper and cook until just hot. During the last minute, add the kale and spinach and stir until wilted.

2. While the vegetables are cooking, heat a large (4- to 6-quart) saucepan of water over high heat until boiling. Add the chickpea pasta and cook according to the package directions (7 to 9 minutes) until tender.

3. Drain the pasta. (If the sauce is too thick, retain a little pasta water to thin it out.) Toss with the vegetables and tomato sauce. Serve.

VARIATION TIP: Chickpea pasta adds fiber and protein to this meal, but feel free to swap it out for the pasta of your choice!

PER SERVING (1 CUP PASTA WITH 1 CUP VEGETABLES AND SAUCE): Calories: 334; Total fat: 7g; Saturated fat: 1g; Cholesterol: 0mg; Sodium: 53mg; Carbohydrates: 51g; Fiber: 12g; Sugar: 12g; Protein: 18g

Apple Acorn Squash

Serves 2 **Prep Time:** 10 minutes **Cook Time:** 30 minutes

Make this dish on a fall night and pair it with a glass of red zinfandel or merlot. Red wine is a rich source of polyphenols, powerful antioxidants that may protect the brain by interfering with amyloid protein plaque formation. One 5-ounce glass of red wine a day is a part of the MIND diet.

1 small acorn squash

1 tablespoon extra-virgin olive oil, divided

½ cup sliced leeks, rinsed well, white part only

½ apple, cored and chopped (Honeycrisp or Gala work best)

½ cup cooked brown rice

½ cup cooked brown lentils

⅛ teaspoon cayenne pepper

¼ teaspoon cinnamon

1 tablespoon maple syrup

1 cup chopped Tuscan kale

2 tablespoons dried cranberries

2 tablespoons chopped raw, unsalted pistachios

1. Preheat the oven to 425°F. Line a rimmed baking sheet with aluminum foil.

2. Cut the squash in half lengthwise, then scoop out the seeds. Drizzle each half with ½ teaspoon of olive oil and place the squash cut-side down on the baking sheet. Roast for 25 to 30 minutes, until the squash is soft when pierced with a fork.

3. While the squash is roasting, in a medium skillet, heat the remaining 2 teaspoons of olive oil and add the leeks and apple. Sauté for 5 minutes, until the apple is just slightly softened. Stir in the brown rice, lentils, cayenne, cinnamon, and maple syrup and toss until well combined. Add the kale and cranberries and heat for 2 to 3 minutes, just until the rice and lentils are hot and the kale has wilted.

4. Once the squash is done, remove it from the oven and transfer it to two plates. Add 1 cup of the rice and lentil mixture to each half, top each with 1 tablespoon of pistachios, and serve.

PER SERVING (½ SQUASH WITH 1 CUP FILLING): Calories: 369; Total fat: 11g; Saturated fat: 2g; Cholesterol: 0mg; Sodium: 17mg; Carbohydrates: 63g; Fiber: 11g; Sugar: 13g; Protein: 10g

Gnocchi and Spring Vegetables

Serves 2 **Prep Time:** 10 minutes **Cook Time:** 15 minutes

Using premade gnocchi, made without eggs and cheese, turns this recipe into a quick and easy vegan dinner for two.

1 teaspoon extra-virgin olive oil

¼ cup chopped onion

1 teaspoon minced garlic

2 tablespoons tomato paste

1 (15-ounce) can tomato sauce

½ teaspoon dried basil

¼ teaspoon dried oregano

½ teaspoon dried parsley, or 1 teaspoon finely chopped fresh parsley

¼ teaspoon freshly ground black pepper

2 canned artichoke hearts, quartered

2 cups packed fresh baby spinach

1 cup (1-inch) asparagus pieces

8 ounces plain gnocchi

1. In a large skillet, heat the olive oil over medium-low heat. Add the onion and sauté for 3 minutes, or until translucent. Add the garlic and sauté for 1 minute, being careful not to burn it.

2. Add the tomato paste to the onion and garlic and stir for 1 minute to thoroughly combine. Add the tomato sauce, basil, oregano, parsley, and pepper. Stir to combine well and cook for 7 minutes. During the last minute or two, add the artichokes and spinach, and stir until the spinach is wilted.

3. While the tomato sauce is cooking, bring a large saucepan of water to a boil over high heat. Add the asparagus pieces and gnocchi to the water and boil until the gnocchi floats to the top, 2 to 5 minutes, depending on the size of the gnocchi. Drain, then add to the pan with the pan with the tomato sauce and toss the asparagus and gnocchi to coat well.

4. Divide between two plates and serve with some crusty bread and a side salad if desired.

COOKING TIP: If using thick asparagus, add it to the water 1 to 2 minutes before adding the gnocchi to give it enough time to cook.

PER SERVING: Calories: 342; Total fat: 11g; Saturated fat: 5g; Cholesterol: 18mg; Sodium: 539mg; Carbohydrates: 60g; Fiber: 16g; Sugar: 14g; Protein: 14g

Stuffed Banana Peppers

Serves 2 **Prep Time:** 15 minutes **Cook Time:** 30 minutes

In these vegan stuffed peppers, the black beans, quinoa, and corn add protein and fiber, making this dish rich in flavor and MIND diet friendly.

1 cup Zesty Tomato Sauce (page 110)

½ teaspoon Southwest Seasoning Blend (page 111)

3 large banana peppers (about 6 inches long)

½ cup cooked quinoa

¼ cup reduced-sodium black beans, drained and rinsed

¼ cup fresh, frozen, or canned (no salt added) yellow corn

¼ cup finely chopped red bell pepper

½ teaspoon minced jalapeño pepper

3 tablespoons Spicy Avocado Dressing (page 108)

1. Preheat the oven to 350°F.

2. In a small bowl, combine the tomato sauce with the southwest seasoning blend and set aside.

3. Slice the banana peppers in half lengthwise and clean out the seeds and membranes. Set aside.

4. In a medium bowl, combine the quinoa, black beans, corn, bell pepper, and jalapeño pepper. Add ¾ cup of the tomato sauce and mix well to combine.

5. Spread the remaining ¼ cup of tomato sauce on the bottom of a 9-by-9-inch baking dish. Lay the stuffed pepper halves on top of the sauce, trying not to overlap them. Fill the 6 halves with the quinoa filling, dividing it evenly among all the stuffed peppers.

6. Cover the pan tightly with aluminum foil and bake for 25 to 30 minutes, until the sauce is bubbling and the banana peppers are tender.

7. Top the stuffed peppers with some of the sauce from the bottom of the pan, along with a dollop of the avocado dressing, and serve.

USE IT AGAIN: Make extra quinoa and use it later in the week for the Orange Quinoa-Chickpea Salad (page 38).

PER SERVING (3 PEPPER HALVES): Calories: 197; Total fat: 4g; Saturated fat: 1g; Cholesterol: 0mg; Sodium: 76mg; Carbohydrates: 36g; Fiber: 11g; Sugar: 8g; Protein: 9g

Baked Falafel Pita Pockets with Tabbouleh

Serves 2 **Prep Time:** 10 minutes **Cook Time:** 25 minutes

Traditionally a part of casual Mediterranean cuisine, falafel are deep-fried fritters made with chickpeas, parsley, and lemon. The falafel in this dish are baked, but they still have a nice crisp outside and a tender interior. Authentic tabbouleh is an herb salad made with parsley and mint and a little bulgur wheat. I make mine with more bulgur, lots of vegetables and herbs, and lightly season it with a lemon dressing.

FOR THE FALAFEL

1 cup canned chickpeas, drained and rinsed

½ cup cooked bulgur wheat

¼ cup chopped yellow onion

¼ cup coarsely chopped fresh flat-leaf parsley (leaves and thin stems)

¼ cup coarsely chopped fresh cilantro (leaves and stems)

1 tablespoon freshly squeezed lemon juice

½ teaspoon ground cumin

¼ teaspoon red pepper flakes

1 tablespoon extra-virgin olive oil

1 (6-inch) pita bread, halved

2 tablespoons Tahini Dressing (page 107) ▶

TO MAKE THE FALAFEL

1. Preheat the oven to 425°F. Line a baking sheet with aluminum foil.

2. In the bowl of a food processor, place the chickpeas, bulgur, onion, parsley, cilantro, lemon juice, cumin, and red pepper flakes. Process until the mixture is well combined, but not pureed, and holds together when squeezed.

3. Form the mixture into 6 small patties and place them on the foil-lined baking sheet.

4. Brush both sides of each patty with the olive oil and bake for 12 minutes. Turn the patties over and bake for 12 minutes more, or until crisp on the outside. Remove from the oven and allow to cool slightly.

5. Gently pull open each half of the pita bread to form a pocket. Place 3 patties in each pita pocket half. Drizzle with the tahini dressing.

FOR THE TABBOULEH

1 cup cooked bulgur
  wheat

½ cup minced fresh curly
  parsley (leaves and
  stems)

2 tablespoons minced
  fresh mint leaves

½ cup finely chopped
  cucumber

½ cup finely chopped
  tomato (seeds removed)

2 tablespoons sliced
  scallions, white and
  green parts

2 tablespoons extra-virgin
  olive oil

2 tablespoons freshly
  squeezed lemon juice

⅛ teaspoon kosher salt

¼ teaspoon freshly
  ground black pepper

TO MAKE THE TABBOULEH

6. While the falafel are cooking, in a medium bowl, combine the bulgur, parsley, mint, cucumber, tomato, and scallions.

7. In a small bowl whisk together the olive oil, lemon juice, salt, and pepper. Pour the lemon and oil dressing into the bulgur mixture and combine well. Serve the tabbouleh alongside the pita pockets. (Tabbouleh can be made up to a day ahead.)

COOKING TIP: While some herbs need to be stripped from their stems, that isn't necessary when using parsley and cilantro. The stems of these plants are flavorful and add some nice crunch and texture, which is perfect in the tabbouleh and falafel.

PER SERVING (1 PITA POCKET WITH 1 CUP TABBOULEH):
Calories: 592; Total fat: 27g; Saturated fat: 4g; Cholesterol: 0mg; Sodium: 357mg; Carbohydrates: 74g; Fiber: 16g; Sugar: 8g; Protein: 17g

Butternut Squash and Barley Risotto with Baby Kale

Serves 2 **Prep Time:** 10 minutes **Cook Time:** 35 minutes

Risotto is one of my all-time favorite comfort foods. This recipe is mostly hands-off, making it a perfect low-maintenance meal for two.

1 small butternut squash

2 teaspoons extra-virgin olive oil

½ cup finely chopped sweet onion

½ cup pearled barley

½ cup white wine

2 cups Homemade Vegetable Broth (page 109)

1 cup baby kale

1 teaspoon chopped fresh sage leaves

VARIATION TIP: Add other greens like baby spinach, Swiss chard, or arugula to add extra veggies to this dish, or serve a hearty green salad on the side.

1. Cut small slits in all sides of the squash. Place the squash in a microwave-safe dish and microwave for 5 to 7 minutes, until it is just soft and can be easily pierced with a fork. Remove the squash from the microwave and set it aside to cool.

2. While the squash is cooling, in a medium skillet, heat the olive oil over medium heat. Add the onion and cook for 3 minutes, until just softened.

3. Add the barley and cook over medium heat for 1 minute, stirring to coat with the olive oil and combine with the onion. Add the wine and stir quickly to combine. Cook for 1 to 2 minutes, until most of the liquid is gone.

4. Once the squash is cooled, cut the top off and split it in half. Scoop the seeds out of the center, then scoop out the squash and dice it.

5. Add the broth to the skillet and bring to a boil. Stir in the squash, cover, reduce the heat to low, and simmer for 15 to 20 minutes, until all liquid has been absorbed. Add the kale during the last minute of cooking to wilt. Divide between two plates, garnish with the sage leaves, and serve.

PER SERVING (2 CUPS): Calories: 426; Total fat: 6g; Saturated fat: 1g; Cholesterol: 0mg; Sodium: 26mg; Carbohydrates: 92g; Fiber: 17g; Sugar: 12g; Protein: 10g

Spaghetti Squash and Mushroom Bolognese

Serves 2 **Prep Time:** 15 minutes **Cook Time:** 45 minutes

Once cooked, minced cremini mushrooms have the texture of ground beef in this mushroom "Bolognese" sauce.

1 small spaghetti squash

1 tablespoon extra-virgin olive oil, divided

¾ cup chopped carrots

2 cups finely chopped cremini mushrooms

1½ cups Zesty Tomato Sauce (page 110)

½ teaspoon dried basil

¼ teaspoon dried oregano

¼ teaspoon garlic powder

COOKING TIP: To test the squash to see if it is done, remove it from the oven and flip it over. Run a fork along the edge. If the squash is done, it should easily pull away from the sides.

1. Preheat the oven to 425°F. Line a small baking sheet with parchment paper.

2. Cut the squash in half lengthwise. Scoop out the seeds and rub the interior with 1 teaspoon of olive oil. Pierce the outsides with a fork, and place the squash cut-side down on the prepared baking sheet.

3. Roast for 30 minutes. Test with a fork and when tender, carefully remove from the oven. (See tip for how to test for doneness.)

4. While the squash is cooking, in a medium skillet, heat the remaining 2 teaspoons of olive oil. Add the carrots and cook for 2 to 3 minutes over medium heat. Stir in the mushrooms and cook for 5 minutes, or until the liquid from the mushrooms is absorbed.

5. Stir in the tomato sauce, basil, oregano, and garlic powder and cook for about 5 minutes, until the sauce is slightly thickened.

6. With a fork, pull the noodle-like strands from the squash and divide the squash between two plates. Top each with half the mushroom Bolognese sauce and serve with a side salad.

PER SERVING: Calories: 263; Total fat: 9g; Saturated fat: 1g; Cholesterol: 0mg; Sodium: 142mg; Carbohydrates: 46g; Fiber: 10g; Sugar: 21g; Protein: 7g

Soba Noodles with Spicy Peanut Sauce

Serves 2 **Prep Time:** 10 minutes **Cook Time:** 10 minutes

This dish is packed with flavor and MIND-diet friendly ingredients. Edamame is one of the few vegetables that is a complete protein with all the essential amino acids necessary for the growth and development of the neurotransmitters in the brain's communication system. Soba noodles are usually made with a blend of buckwheat and wheat flour. Buckwheat is rich in fiber and contains flavonoids that may have a role in reducing inflammation.

FOR THE PEANUT SAUCE

¼ cup creamy peanut butter

1 tablespoon soy sauce

1 teaspoon lime zest

1 tablespoon lime juice

½ teaspoon toasted sesame oil

½ teaspoon red pepper flakes

½ teaspoon freshly grated ginger or ginger powder ▶

TO MAKE THE PEANUT SAUCE

1. In a medium bowl, whisk together the peanut butter, soy sauce, lime zest, lime juice, sesame oil, red pepper flakes, and ginger until well blended. Set aside.

TO MAKE THE SOBA NOODLES AND VEGETABLES

2. In a medium skillet, heat the olive oil over medium heat. Add the carrots, bell pepper, and edamame. Cook for 2 minutes, until just hot. Add the scallions and stir for 30 seconds. Remove from the heat.

3. In a large saucepan, bring 6 to 8 cups of water to a boil over high heat. Add the soba noodles and cook according to the package directions (4 to 5 minutes) until just al dente. Drain and put the noodles back in the saucepan.

1 teaspoon extra-virgin
olive oil

½ cup shredded carrots

½ cup thinly sliced red
bell pepper strips

1 cup shelled edamame
(thawed, if frozen)

2 tablespoons sliced
scallions, white and
green parts

6 ounces soba noodles

¼ cup shredded red
cabbage

¼ cup peanuts, chopped

2 tablespoons chopped
cilantro

4. Immediately toss the soba noodles with the
peanut sauce to coat. Add the cooked vegetables
and toss well.

5. Divide between two plates and top with the cabbage, peanuts, and cilantro.

VARIATION TIP: Soba noodles are commonly found in the international section of most grocery stores. If you can't find soba noodles, spaghetti noodles are a good substitute.

PER SERVING: Calories: 737; Total fat: 34g; Saturated fat: 6g; Cholesterol: 0mg; Sodium: 1,151mg; Carbohydrates: 88g; Fiber: 9g; Sugar: 9g; Protein: 34g

CHAPTER 5

Fish and Seafood

Tilapia Fish Tacos

Serves 2 **Prep Time:** 15 minutes **Cook Time:** 5 minutes

Tilapia is a light whitefish that is low in fat and sodium and rich in protein. It is also a good source of vitamin B12, which is important for keeping the brain's communication system working. These easy tacos are perfect for a busy weeknight.

1 cup shredded Napa cabbage

¼ cup shredded red cabbage

2 tablespoons diced red onion

Avocado oil cooking spray

6 (6-inch) flour tortillas

2 (4-ounce) tilapia fillets

½ tablespoon Southwest Seasoning Blend (page 111)

1 tablespoon coarsely chopped fresh cilantro leaves

1 avocado, pitted, peeled, and chopped (optional)

Spicy Avocado Dressing (page 108), for drizzling

1 lime, cut into 6 pieces, for serving

1. In a medium bowl, combine the Napa cabbage, red cabbage, and red onion. Set aside.

2. Heat a grill pan over medium-high heat. Coat the pan with the cooking spray.

3. Place the tortillas in the pan and grill on each side for about 1 minute, or until grill marks appear. Transfer the tortillas to a plate and set aside.

4. Cut the tilapia fillets into ½-inch-by-1-inch pieces. Place the tilapia pieces in a medium bowl and toss with the southwest seasoning to coat.

5. Place the tilapia pieces on the grill pan and grill for 2 minutes per side, or until flaky. To keep the fish from falling apart, pat it dry with a paper towel before placing it on the hot grill pan. Turn the fish with a long thin spatula once while cooking. (It cooks quickly, so watch it closely.)

6. Assemble the tacos. Place about ¼ cup of the cabbage mixture on top of each tortilla. Divide the tilapia pieces, cilantro, and avocado (if using) evenly among the tortillas. Serve with a lime wedge on the side.

VARIATION TIP: Cod, salmon, and mahi-mahi also work well in tacos!

PER SERVING (3 TACOS): Calories: 389; Total fat: 7g; Saturated fat: 2g; Cholesterol: 57mg; Sodium: 601mg; Carbohydrates: 50g; Fiber: 4g; Sugar: 5g; Protein: 31g

Honey-Mustard Salmon

Serves 2 **Prep Time:** 10 minutes **Cook Time:** 10 minutes

Salmon is an easy fish to cook and an excellent source of omega-3 fatty acids, vitamin D, and B vitamins—all important nutrients for the brain! The Dijon mustard adds a sweet and tangy flavor to every bite of the buttery salmon. Serve it with a side of roasted asparagus or on top of a leafy green salad.

3 ½ teaspoons Dijon mustard

2 ½ teaspoons honey

⅛ teaspoon dried thyme

2 teaspoons extra-virgin olive oil

2 (5-ounce) skin-on salmon fillets

⅛ teaspoon freshly ground black pepper

1. In a small bowl, mix the mustard, honey, and thyme together until well combined. Set aside.

2. Heat a medium skillet over medium heat. When hot, pour in the olive oil and heat for 1 minute, turning the pan to coat. Season the salmon fillets with the pepper and place them in the hot skillet, skin-side down. Cook the fillets for 5 to 10 minutes (depending on the thickness of the fish), until flaky and the internal temperature reaches 145°F. Top each fillet with 1 tablespoon of the honey-mustard dressing and cook for 1 minute.

3. Carefully remove the fillets from the skillet. Top each with any remaining dressing.

COOKING TIP: To gauge the cooking time for the fish, measure the fillet at the thickest part and estimate it will take 10 minutes per inch. For thicker fillets, turn the fish over halfway through the cooking time.

PER SERVING: Calories: 279; Total fat: 13g; Saturated fat: 2g; Cholesterol: 64mg; Sodium: 162mg; Carbohydrates: 8g; Fiber: 0g; Sugar: 7g; Protein: 31g

Pesto Spaghetti with Scallops and Broccoli

Serves 2 **Prep Time:** 10 minutes **Cook Time:** 20 minutes

I love scallops because they are easy to prepare and cook quickly. They are also jam-packed with brain-healthy nutrients like vitamin B12, zinc, and omega-3 fatty acids, making them an ideal choice for the MIND diet. This light dish is elevated enough for a special occasion or perfect for date night. For the best timing, cook the pasta and broccoli at the same time, and sear the scallops last.

FOR THE BROCCOLI

2 cups broccoli florets

2 teaspoons extra-virgin olive oil

½ teaspoon freshly ground black pepper

1 teaspoon lemon zest

1 teaspoon freshly squeezed lemon juice

FOR THE PESTO SPAGHETTI AND SCALLOPS

4 ounces spaghetti

3 tablespoons Pesto Sauce (page 106)

2 teaspoons grapeseed oil

8 ounces sea scallops

⅛ teaspoon kosher salt

¼ teaspoon freshly ground black pepper

TO MAKE THE BROCCOLI

1. Preheat the oven to 425°F. Line a baking sheet with aluminum foil.

2. In a medium bowl, toss the broccoli florets with the olive oil and pepper. Spread them out on the prepared baking sheet, place the sheet in the middle of the oven, and roast for 15 minutes, or until the broccoli is tender and just lightly browned.

3. Remove from the oven and toss quickly with the lemon zest and lemon juice. Set aside.

TO MAKE THE PESTO SPAGHETTI AND SCALLOPS

4. Bring a large stockpot of water to a boil over high heat. Add the pasta and cook for 8 to 10 minutes, or until al dente. Drain the pasta and toss it with the pesto sauce.

5. While the pasta is cooking, heat the grapeseed oil in a cast-iron pan over medium-high heat until it is very hot.

6. Season each side of the scallops with the salt and pepper. Place the scallops in the pan and brown them on both sides, about 2 minutes per side, turning them when they easily pull away from the pan.

7. Top the pasta with the scallops and serve with the broccoli on the side.

COOKING TIP: Grapeseed oil has a high smoke point and will hold up to the high temperature required for cooking the scallops better than olive oil will. To get that beautiful sear on the scallops, be sure to heat the pan and the oil to a high temperature before placing the scallops in the pan. Once they are in the pan, let them sit undisturbed until you have to turn them. This gives them time to cook and develop its beautiful brown color.

PER SERVING: Calories: 528; Total fat: 24g; Saturated fat: 4g; Cholesterol: 31mg; Sodium: 612mg; Carbohydrates: 53g; Fiber: 4g; Sugar: 3g; Protein: 26g

Sesame-Ginger Shrimp Sliders with Sweet Potato Wedges

Serves 2 **Prep Time:** 15 minutes **Cook Time:** 25 minutes

It's common to think that only plant foods contain antioxidants, but the antioxidant astaxanthin is found in shrimp and is responsible for its pink color. Astaxanthin has been found to have anti-inflammatory properties and is being studied for its potential to protect cognitive health.

FOR THE SWEET POTATO WEDGES

1 large sweet potato (about 10 ounces)

1 teaspoon avocado oil

1 teaspoon Chinese five-spice powder

FOR THE SHRIMP SLIDERS

8 ounces shrimp, peeled and deveined

1 egg

¼ cup finely chopped yellow onion

1 tablespoon chopped fresh ginger

1 teaspoon toasted sesame oil

1 tablespoon lime juice

1 tablespoon chopped fresh cilantro

¼ cup finely chopped red bell pepper ▶

TO MAKE THE SWEET POTATO WEDGES

1. Preheat the oven to 425°F. Line a baking sheet with aluminum foil, then place it in the oven to preheat.

2. Cut the sweet potato into 8 wedges. In a medium bowl, toss the sweet potato wedges with the avocado oil to coat well. Sprinkle with the five-spice powder and toss again.

3. Remove the hot baking sheet from the oven and place the potato wedges on it. Roast the potatoes for 20 to 25 minutes, flipping them halfway through the cooking time.

TO MAKE THE SHRIMP SLIDERS

4. While the sweet potatoes are roasting, make the sliders. In the bowl of a food processor, place the shrimp, egg, onion, ginger, sesame oil, lime juice, and cilantro. Pulse until combined and the shrimp is well chopped, but not pureed.

5. Place the shrimp mixture in a medium bowl and add the bell pepper, salt, and bread crumbs. Combine well. Allow the mixture to sit for about 5 minutes to give the bread crumbs time to hydrate.

⅛ teaspoon kosher salt

¼ cup panko bread crumbs

2 teaspoons avocado oil

4 whole wheat slider buns

Spicy Avocado Dressing (page 108) (optional)

4 lettuce leaves

6. Form 4 (¼-cup) patties with the shrimp mixture. In a medium skillet, heat the avocado oil over medium-high heat. Once the oil is hot, add the shrimp patties. Press down on each slightly to make a 1-inch-thick patty. Cook for about 1 minute, then flip the patties and cook the other side for 1 minute more, until the patty is cooked through or reaches an internal temperature of 120°F. Transfer the patties from the skillet to a plate.

7. On the bottom of each slider bun, spread some avocado dressing (if using) and add a piece of lettuce. Add a shrimp patty and top with the other half of the bun. Serve with sweet potato wedges on the side.

COOKING TIP: Avocado oil has a high smoke point and has a similar nutritional profile to olive oil. It has also been shown to help reduce LDL (bad) cholesterol levels and inflammation.

PER SERVING (2 SLIDERS AND 4 POTATO WEDGES): Calories: 463; Total fat: 15g; Saturated fat: 3g; Cholesterol: 276mg; Sodium: 609mg; Carbohydrates: 51g; Fiber: 8g; Sugar: 10g; Protein: 33g

Pecan-Crusted Trout with Apple-Rice Blend

Serves 2 **Prep Time:** 20 minutes **Cook Time:** 1 hour

Trout is a protein-rich source of omega-3 fatty acids, vitamin D, B vitamins, and the antioxidant selenium. All these nutrients are an important part of the MIND diet and help support the immune system, reduce inflammation, and maintain brain health. A sweeter apple, such as Gala or Honeycrisp, will complement the date and orange flavors and lend a bit of crunch.

FOR THE APPLE-RICE BLEND

1 cup water

⅓ cup wild rice blend

2 teaspoons extra-virgin olive oil

2 tablespoons thinly sliced celery

¼ small sweet onion, chopped

½ apple, chopped

¼ cup chopped dates

2 tablespoons chopped pecans

1 teaspoon orange zest ▶

TO MAKE THE APPLE-RICE BLEND

1. In a small saucepan over high heat, bring the water to a boil. Add the rice, reduce the heat to low, and simmer, covered, for 45 to 50 minutes, or until all the water is absorbed. Set aside. (You can make the rice up to 2 days ahead of time and store it in the refrigerator until you are ready to use it.)

2. In a medium skillet, heat the olive oil over medium-low heat. Add the celery, onion, and apple and sauté for 5 minutes, or until the apple is just softened. Add the dates, pecans, and orange zest and cook, stirring, for 1 minute. Add the apple mixture to the warm rice and stir to combine.

TO MAKE THE TROUT

3. Season the trout with the pepper.

4. Place the flour in a small tray or plate. Coat each fillet on both sides with the flour.

5. Place the egg in a small, shallow bowl and coat each fillet with it.

FOR THE TROUT

2 (5-ounce) skin-on trout
fillets

¼ teaspoon freshly
ground black pepper

¼ cup all-purpose flour

1 egg, beaten

¼ cup finely chopped
pecans

1 tablespoon extra-virgin
olive oil

6. Cover the top of the skinless side of each fillet with 2 tablespoons of pecans, and gently press the pecans into the trout.

7. In a large skillet, heat the olive oil over medium heat. Add the trout fillets, skin-side down, and cook for about 3 minutes. Carefully flip each fillet over and cook for 1 to 2 minutes more on the pecan-crusted side. Remove carefully and serve skin-side down.

8. Serve with the apple-rice blend on the side.

COOKING TIP: Make sure to really press the pecans into the trout before cooking so they stick to the fish and don't fall off when you flip the fillets.

PER SERVING: Calories: 641; Total fat: 30g; Saturated fat: 4g; Cholesterol: 175mg; Sodium: 119mg; Carbohydrates: 55g; Fiber: 7g; Sugar: 18g; Protein: 40g

Spicy Tomatoes and Shrimp with Zoodles

Serves 2 **Prep Time:** 10 minutes **Cook Time:** 15 minutes

I always have shrimp in my freezer because it is so quick to prepare. To thaw, just run the shrimp under cold water for a few minutes, and it's ready to go. This recipe also uses frozen zoodles (zucchini noodles) for a super quick, tasty, and brain-healthy weeknight dinner.

2 teaspoons extra-virgin olive oil

¼ cup finely chopped yellow onion

1 teaspoon minced garlic

⅛ teaspoon dried basil

¼ teaspoon red pepper flakes

⅛ teaspoon kosher salt

1 (15-ounce) can petite diced tomatoes, undrained

8 ounces extra-large shrimp, peeled and deveined

1 (12-ounce) package zucchini noodles

1. In a medium skillet, heat the olive oil over medium heat. Add the onion and cook for 3 minutes, until just beginning to soften. Add the garlic, basil, red pepper flakes, and salt and cook for 1 minute, until fragrant. Add the tomatoes with their juices and boil for 5 minutes, until the liquid is reduced and the sauce is thickened. (If you like a spicier sauce, add more red pepper flakes.)

2. Add the shrimp to the tomato mixture and cook, undisturbed, for 2 minutes. Turn each shrimp over, add the zoodles, and cook for 1 to 2 minutes, until the zoodles are heated through and the shrimp is pink and cooked through.

VARIATION TIP: If you want to make your own zoodles, you don't need a spiralizer. Cut the ends off of the zucchini and use a vegetable peeler to cut the zucchini lengthwise in long slices. Then, stack a few slices together and make long, thin cuts to form "noodles."

PER SERVING: Calories: 193; Total fat: 7g; Saturated fat: 1g; Cholesterol: 143mg; Sodium: 833mg; Carbohydrates: 16g; Fiber: 6g; Sugar: 10g; Protein: 19g

Lemony Sole and Orzo

Serves 2 **Prep Time:** 10 minutes **Cook Time:** 15 minutes

Sole is low in fat, and the fat it has is polyunsaturated, which contains brain-supporting omega-3 fatty acids. I love this meal because it looks elegant but comes together in about 30 minutes.

FOR THE ORZO

2 cups water or
   Homemade Vegetable
   Broth (page 109)

½ cup orzo

1 tablespoon freshly
   squeezed lemon juice

1 teaspoon extra-virgin
   olive oil

Fresh basil, finely
   chopped, for garnish

FOR THE SOLE

2 teaspoons extra-virgin
   olive oil

1 teaspoon butter

2 (5-ounce) sole fillets

⅛ teaspoon freshly
   ground black pepper

½ teaspoon lemon zest

¼ cup freshly squeezed
   lemon juice

TO MAKE THE ORZO

1. In a small saucepan over high heat, bring the water or broth to a boil. Add the orzo, reduce the heat to low, and simmer, covered, for 10 to 15 minutes, until the orzo is tender. Drain.

2. Fluff the orzo with a fork, add the lemon juice and olive oil, and toss to combine. Garnish with the fresh basil.

TO MAKE THE SOLE

3. While the orzo is cooking, in a medium skillet, heat the olive oil and butter over medium heat.

4. Season the sole with the pepper and sprinkle with the lemon zest. Gently place the fillets in the skillet and add the lemon juice. Cook for 3 to 5 minutes, until the sole is flaky. Carefully transfer the fish from the skillet to a plate.

5. Bring the remaining sauce to a low boil and cook for 2 to 3 minutes, until silky and slightly thickened. Pour the sauce over the fish. Serve with the orzo and a salad on the side.

VARIATION TIP: The butter gives this sauce a creamier texture, but you can eliminate it if you prefer. If sole is unavailable, flounder or haddock are good substitutions.

PER SERVING: Calories: 347; Total fat: 12g; Saturated fat: 3g; Cholesterol: 69mg; Sodium: 420mg; Carbohydrates: 36g; Fiber: 2g; Sugar: 1g; Protein: 23g

Salmon and Spinach Linguini

Serves 2 **Prep Time:** 15 minutes **Cook Time:** 30 minutes

This easy dish is the perfect blend of zesty and creamy flavors with a bright, fresh note from the lemon juice and dill.

4 ounces spinach linguini

1 (8-ounce) skinless salmon fillet

⅛ teaspoon kosher salt

¼ teaspoon freshly ground black pepper

1 tablespoon extra-virgin olive oil

1 cup sliced cremini mushrooms

1 large garlic clove, peeled and crushed

2 tablespoons dry white wine

2 scallions, green part only, thinly sliced

6 grape tomatoes, halved

2 canned artichoke hearts, quartered

2 teaspoons capers, drained and rinsed

2 tablespoons chopped fresh dill

1½ teaspoons freshly squeezed lemon juice

1. Bring a pot of water to boil over high heat and cook the linguini according to the package directions, 7 to 9 minutes. Drain well.

2. Cut the salmon into ¾-inch pieces and season it with the salt and pepper.

3. In a medium skillet, heat the olive oil over medium heat. Cook the salmon pieces for 3 to 4 minutes, flip them over, and cook for 3 to 4 minutes more, until browned. Using a slotted spoon or spatula, transfer the salmon to a plate and tent with aluminum foil to keep it warm.

4. Place the mushrooms in the skillet and cook for 5 to 6 minutes, until browned. Add the garlic and sauté for 30 seconds. Add the wine and cook for 1 minute.

5. Mix in the scallions, tomatoes, artichokes, and capers. Cook for about 5 minutes, until the mushrooms and scallions are tender and the tomatoes are blistered.

6. Add the cooked linguini, salmon, dill, and lemon juice to the mushroom and tomato mixture, toss together carefully to avoid breaking up the salmon, and serve.

PER SERVING: Calories: 541; Total fat: 16g; Saturated fat: 3g; Cholesterol: 51mg; Sodium: 541mg; Carbohydrates: 65g; Fiber: 12g; Sugar: 5g; Protein: 39g

Stuffed Flounder with Grain Salad

Serves 2 **Prep Time:** 15 minutes **Cook Time:** 15 minutes

Flounder is a mild fish that absorbs the flavors of the other ingredients. The wine and lemon juice add tons of flavor to the fish, and the spinach and mushroom stuffing lend a bit of heartiness. To make the lentils and brown rice, see the Eggplant with Tahini Dressing recipe on page 46.

2 teaspoons extra-virgin olive oil

¼ cup sliced leeks, rinsed well, white part only

1 cup chopped cremini mushrooms

2 cups chopped fresh spinach

1 teaspoon finely chopped fresh rosemary

1 tablespoon Dijon mustard

¼ teaspoon freshly ground black pepper

2 (6-ounce) skinless flounder fillets

1 cup white wine

½ teaspoon lemon zest

2 teaspoons freshly squeezed lemon juice

2 cups prepared lentils and brown rice (page 46)

1. In a medium skillet, heat the olive oil over medium heat. Add the leeks and cook, stirring, for about 2 minutes, until softened. Add the mushrooms and cook for 3 to 5 minutes, then stir in the spinach and rosemary and cook until the spinach has wilted. Stir in the Dijon mustard and pepper, transfer to a bowl, and set aside.

2. On a cutting board, lay the flounder fillets flat and spread half the spinach and mushroom mixture down the middle of each fillet. Fold the fillet over to enclose the filling. (You can secure the fish with a toothpick if desired.)

3. Wipe out the skillet with a paper towel. Place it over medium heat and pour in the wine, lemon zest, and lemon juice.

4. Place the fillets in the lemon-wine mixture. Cook, covered, for 5 minutes. Remove from the skillet and serve with 1 cup of lentils and brown rice.

PER SERVING: Calories: 506; Total fat: 10g; Saturated fat: 2g; Cholesterol: 77mg; Sodium: 631mg; Carbohydrates: 50g; Fiber: 11g; Sugar: 5g; Protein: 35g

Poached Cod with Tomatoes and Beans over Polenta

Serves 2 **Prep Time:** 15 minutes **Cook Time:** 15 minutes

This recipe is inspired by a poached cod meal my husband and I had on a recent trip to the East Coast. That dish had Portuguese sausage, which I left out of this recipe, but you could certainly add it for an extra-special treat.

FOR THE COD

2 teaspoons extra-virgin olive oil

¼ cup chopped sweet onion

1 tablespoon minced garlic

¼ teaspoon red pepper flakes

¾ cup canned cannellini beans, drained and rinsed

1 cup petite diced tomatoes, undrained

¼ cup red wine

¾ cup chopped curly kale

2 (4-ounce) cod fillets

Fresh basil, finely chopped, for garnish

FOR THE POLENTA

2 cups Homemade Vegetable Broth (page 109)

⅛ teaspoon kosher salt

½ cup polenta or finely ground cornmeal

TO MAKE THE COD

1. In a large skillet, heat the olive oil over medium-low heat. Add the onion and sauté for 4 minutes, until just translucent. Add the garlic and red pepper flakes and sauté for 1 minute.

2. Add the beans, tomatoes with their juices, and the wine to the onion and garlic mixture and cook for 2 to 3 minutes, until just bubbling. Add the kale and cook for 2 to 3 minutes, until softened.

3. Nestle the cod in the tomato sauce, cover, and cook for about 5 minutes, until the cod is flaky.

TO MAKE THE POLENTA

4. While the cod is cooking, in a medium saucepan, pour in the broth and salt and bring to a boil over medium heat. Slowly add the polenta and cook, stirring constantly to prevent lumps, for about 3 minutes, or until it pulls away from the side of the saucepan.

5. Divide the polenta between two plates and top with the cod fillets, sauce, and beans.

PER SERVING: Calories: 393; Total fat: 6g; Saturated fat: 1g; Cholesterol: 53mg; Sodium: 521mg; Carbohydrates: 56g; Fiber: 9g; Sugar: 5g; Protein: 28g

CHAPTER 6

Poultry and Meat Mains

Pesto-Roasted Turkey with Blistered Green Beans and Tomatoes

Serves 2 **Prep Time:** 5 minutes **Cook Time:** 25 minutes

Brushing the turkey with pesto adds a savory garlic flavor to an otherwise bland turkey breast cutlet and a bit of zip to the green beans and tomatoes. Make it on a rimmed baking sheet for an easy one-dish meal that's simple to clean up. For a heartier dinner, cook fingerling potatoes alongside the turkey and vegetables.

1 teaspoon extra-virgin olive oil

1 (10-ounce) turkey breast cutlet, sliced in half lengthwise

4 teaspoons Pesto Sauce, divided (page 106)

1 cup fresh green beans, ends trimmed, cut into 2-inch pieces

1 cup grape tomatoes

USE IT AGAIN: I often cook two turkey cutlets and then thinly slice the extra one to use on sandwiches through-out the week. The turkey also makes a wonderful addition to the Hummus and Vegetable Wrap (page 41).

1. Preheat the oven to 425°F. Line a rimmed baking sheet with aluminum foil and lightly coat it with the olive oil.

2. Place the turkey cutlets on one side of the prepared baking sheet. Top each cutlet with 1 teaspoon of the pesto sauce. Spread the pesto over the turkey to cover the top and sides.

3. Place the baking sheet in the oven and roast the turkey for 15 minutes while you prepare the green beans and tomatoes.

4. In a medium bowl, toss the green beans and tomatoes with the remaining 2 teaspoons of pesto sauce. After the turkey has been in the oven for 15 minutes, add the green beans and tomatoes to the other side of the baking sheet and continue roasting for 10 minutes more, or until the turkey registers an internal temperature of 165°F and the tomatoes are blistered and popping.

PER SERVING: Calories: 253; Total fat: 10g; Saturated fat: 2g; Cholesterol: 76mg; Sodium: 184mg; Carbohydrates: 7g; Fiber: 2g; Sugar: 4g; Protein: 35g

Chicken with Brussels Sprouts

Serves 2 **Prep Time:** 10 minutes **Cook Time:** 30 minutes

Brussels sprouts have become a trendy vegetable—and for good reason. Not only are they tasty, but they are also incredibly nutritious. Brussels sprouts belong to the same family as kale, and they have many of the same health-promoting properties. They are an excellent source of vitamin K, vitamin C, and a variety of antioxidants that help reduce free radical damage and inflammation.

1 teaspoon grapeseed oil

2 (5-ounce) bone-in, skin-on chicken thighs

¼ cup sliced shallots

10 ounces halved Brussels sprouts (about 3 cups)

2 teaspoons Dijon mustard

½ teaspoon water

COOKING TIP: Grapeseed oil is used in this recipe because it tolerates the high cooking temperature needed to sear the chicken and roast the Brussels sprouts. It is also high in unsaturated fat and a good substitution for olive oil when cooking at high temperatures.

1. Preheat the oven to 425°F.

2. In a cast-iron pan, heat the grapeseed oil over medium-high heat. Add the chicken thighs, skin-side down, and sear. After 2 to 3 minutes, flip the thighs and brown them on the other side for 2 to 3 minutes more.

3. Add the shallots and Brussels sprouts to the pan, nestling them between the chicken thighs. Place the pan in the oven and roast for about 20 minutes.

4. While the chicken and Brussels sprouts are cooking, in a small bowl, combine the mustard and water.

5. After the Brussels sprouts and chicken have roasted for 20 minutes, drizzle the mustard over the Brussels sprouts and stir to combine. Brush the chicken lightly with any remaining mustard and return the pan to the oven. Cook for 5 minutes more, or until the chicken reaches an internal temperature of 165°F. Serve immediately.

PER SERVING: Calories: 342; Total fat: 22g; Saturated fat: 5g; Cholesterol: 111mg; Sodium: 184mg; Carbohydrates: 15g; Fiber: 6g; Sugar: 4g; Protein: 24g

Sheet-Pan Chicken Fajitas with Strawberry-Mango Salsa

Serves 2 **Prep Time:** 10 minutes **Cook Time:** 15 minutes

Who doesn't love a quick and easy one-pan dinner? These spicy chicken fajitas are just that. The strawberry-mango salsa adds a bright freshness and is a great way to get some brain-boosting antioxidants in your meal.

FOR THE SALSA

½ cup diced fresh strawberries

½ cup diced fresh mango

2 teaspoons minced jalapeño

2 tablespoons chopped red or yellow bell pepper

2 tablespoons chopped red onion

1 teaspoon chopped scallions, green part only

2 teaspoons chopped cilantro

½ teaspoon lime zest

1 teaspoon freshly squeezed lime juice

½ teaspoon honey (optional) ▶

TO MAKE THE SALSA

1. In a glass bowl, toss the salsa ingredients together. Cover and refrigerate until ready to use.

TO MAKE THE FAJITAS

2. Preheat the oven to 425°F. Line a rimmed baking sheet with parchment paper or aluminum foil.

3. In a medium bowl, combine the chicken, bell pepper, and onion. Add the avocado oil and toss to coat everything well. Mix in the southwest seasoning and combine until everything is covered with the spices. Spread out the chicken, bell pepper, and onion on the prepared baking sheet. Place the baking sheet in the middle of the oven and cook for 15 minutes, or until the chicken reaches an internal temperature of 165°F.

FOR THE FAJITAS

8 ounces chicken tenders, cut into strips

½ red bell pepper, cut into strips

½ yellow bell pepper, cut into strips

½ small sweet onion, cut into strips

1 tablespoon avocado oil

2 teaspoons Southwest Seasoning Blend (page 111)

4 (6-inch) whole-grain tortillas

Spicy Avocado Dressing (page 108), for serving (optional)

4. To warm the tortillas, wrap them in aluminum foil and place them in the oven with the chicken for the last 5 minutes of cooking. Place the tortillas flat on plates. Top each tortilla with a quarter of the chicken and bell pepper mixture, a quarter of the salsa, and a drizzle of the avocado dressing (if using).

PER SERVING: Calories: 515; Total fat: 17g; Saturated fat: 5g; Cholesterol: 65mg; Sodium: 482mg; Carbohydrates: 56g; Fiber: 11g; Sugar: 11g; Protein: 35g

Chicken Shawarma with Couscous Salad

Serves 2 **Prep Time:** 20 minutes **Cook Time:** 20 minutes

Shawarma is a traditional Mediterranean dish in which the chicken or lamb is slow roasted on a spit, then shaved and served in a pita with hummus. Although the chicken is not slow roasted in this recipe, the blend of seasonings captures the bold flavors of the original dish.

FOR THE COUSCOUS SALAD

¾ cup water or Homemade Vegetable Broth (page 109)

½ cup pearl couscous

1 teaspoon extra-virgin olive oil

¼ cup chopped red onion

½ cup diced seedless cucumber

½ cup diced tomatoes

1 tablespoon chopped fresh parsley

2 tablespoons chopped almonds

2 tablespoons Tahini Dressing (page 107) ▶

TO MAKE THE COUSCOUS SALAD

1. In a small saucepan over high heat, bring the water or broth to a boil. Add the couscous and olive oil, reduce the heat to low, cover, and simmer for 10 to 12 minutes, or until all the liquid is absorbed. Remove the saucepan from the heat, fluff the couscous with a fork, and set aside to cool.

2. In a medium bowl, stir together the couscous, onion, cucumber, tomatoes, parsley, and almonds until well combined.

3. Stir in the tahini dressing and toss well to coat. Cover and refrigerate the couscous salad until ready to serve. (You can make this up to 1 day in advance.)

TO MAKE THE CHICKEN

4. In a small bowl, combine the cumin, turmeric, paprika, cinnamon, salt, and pepper.

5. On a cutting board, lay out the chicken pieces and cover them on all sides with the spice mixture.

FOR THE CHICKEN

1 teaspoon ground cumin

¼ teaspoon turmeric

¼ teaspoon smoked
  paprika

⅛ teaspoon cinnamon

⅛ teaspoon kosher salt

¼ teaspoon freshly
  ground black pepper

6 ounces chicken tenders,
  cut into strips

2 teaspoons extra-virgin
  olive oil

½ cup Hummus (page 94)

1 (6-inch) pita bread, cut
  into quarters

6. Set a medium skillet over medium heat. Pour in the olive oil. Once hot, add the chicken pieces and brown on all sides, 5 to 7 minutes.

7. Smear ¼ cup of hummus on each plate and top with half the chicken pieces. Serve each plate with half the couscous salad and 2 pita bread quarters.

COOKING TIP: Heat the skillet over medium heat before adding the olive oil. Then add the oil and heat it before adding the chicken. This step will help brown the chicken quickly and prevent it from drying out.

PER SERVING: Calories: 566; Total fat: 17g; Saturated fat: 2g; Cholesterol: 48mg; Sodium: 519mg; Carbohydrates: 69g; Fiber: 8g; Sugar: 3g; Protein: 32g

Spicy Chicken and Rice Skillet

Serves 2 **Prep Time:** 5 minutes **Cook Time:** 25 minutes

Although I love to cook and experiment in the kitchen, there are some nights my husband and I just need to get a meal on the table quickly. This dish is one of my favorites because it is easy, is spicy, uses one pan, and works with almost any vegetable. I use Italian-seasoned chicken sausage and Zesty Tomato Sauce to ramp up the flavor.

1 tablespoon extra-virgin olive oil

½ small yellow onion, chopped

2 Italian-seasoned chicken sausages

½ red bell pepper, chopped

1 small zucchini, cut into ½-inch slices

1 cup cooked brown rice

1 cup Zesty Tomato Sauce (page 110)

½ teaspoon dried basil

½ teaspoon dried oregano

¼ teaspoon garlic powder

¼ teaspoon red pepper flakes

2 cups chopped fresh baby spinach

1. In a large skillet, heat the oil over medium-low heat. Add the onion and cook for 5 minutes, until translucent.

2. While the onion is cooking, slice the sausage into ½-inch-thick slices. Add the sausage, bell pepper, and zucchini to the skillet with the onion. Increase the heat to medium and cook, stirring occasionally, for 10 minutes.

3. Once the zucchini has softened, add the rice, tomato sauce, basil, oregano, garlic powder, and red pepper flakes to the skillet, cover, and cook, stirring occasionally, for 10 minutes. Add the spinach during the last 2 minutes and cook for just long enough to wilt it. Divide between two plates and serve.

VARIATION TIP: This recipe allows you to use up any vegetables you have on hand. Swap the spinach for kale, and mix in peas, summer squash, or eggplant.

PER SERVING: Calories: 346; Total fat: 13g; Saturated fat: 2g; Cholesterol: 43mg; Sodium: 451mg; Carbohydrates: 43g; Fiber: 7g; Sugar: 11g; Protein: 18g

Greek Lamb Kabobs with Couscous Salad

Serves 2 **Prep Time:** 20 minutes, plus 4 to 8 hours to marinate
Cook Time: 10 minutes

Lamb, olive oil, garlic, and mint are classic flavors of Greek cuisine. The Tahini Dressing (page 107) provides a boost of unsaturated fats and antioxidants.

¼ cup extra-virgin olive oil

½ teaspoon lemon zest

¼ cup freshly squeezed lemon juice

½ teaspoon chopped fresh mint leaves

¼ teaspoon chopped fresh oregano

1 teaspoon minced garlic

⅛ teaspoon smoked paprika

⅛ teaspoon kosher salt

¼ teaspoon freshly ground black pepper

8 ounces leg of lamb, cut into 1-inch cubes

½ cup large white or yellow onion slices

Couscous Salad (page 82)

1. In a medium bowl, combine the olive oil, lemon zest, lemon juice, mint, oregano, garlic, paprika, salt, and pepper. Mix well and place in a large resealable plastic bag.

2. Add the lamb cubes to the bag and mix to coat the lamb. Seal the bag and place it in the refrigerator for 4 to 8 hours to marinate.

3. After the lamb is done marinating, heat the grill to 400°F.

4. Thread metal, or wooden skewers that have been soaked in water, with the lamb and onion, alternating pieces of lamb and pieces of onion. Depending on the skewer length, you will have about 4 medium kabobs.

5. Grill the kabobs for about 10 minutes, 5 minutes per side, until the lamb reaches an internal temperature of 145°F for medium-rare.

6. Serve the skewers over the couscous salad.

COOKING TIP: If using wooden skewers, soak them in a pan of warm water for 30 minutes before threading with the lamb and onion to prevent them from burning on the grill.

PER SERVING (2 KABOBS WITH 1 CUP SALAD): Calories: 536; Total fat: 26g; Saturated fat: 5g; Cholesterol: 74mg; Sodium: 240mg; Carbohydrates: 44g; Fiber: 5g; Sugar: 5g; Protein: 32g

Spinach-Stuffed Pork Tenderloin Rolls

Serves 2 **Prep Time:** 20 minutes, plus 10 minutes to rest **Cook Time:** 40 minutes

Pork tenderloin is a small, tender, lean piece of meat that is easily butterflied and pounded thin. This meal is a delicious option for date night. You can also easily double it and serve for company.

4 teaspoons grapeseed oil, divided

2 tablespoons finely chopped sweet onion

1 small garlic clove, minced

4 cups chopped fresh baby spinach

½ teaspoon freshly ground black pepper, divided

1 (8-ounce) pork tenderloin

2 tablespoons Pesto Sauce (page 106)

1. Preheat the oven to 425°F.

2. In a medium skillet, heat 2 teaspoons of the grapeseed oil over medium heat. Add the onion and sauté for 5 minutes, until softened. Add the garlic and cook, stirring constantly, for 1 minute. Stir in the spinach and cook for about 2 minutes, until the spinach is wilted. Season with ¼ teaspoon of pepper, set aside, and let the mixture cool.

3. Meanwhile, butterfly the pork tenderloin. Make a slit lengthwise down the center of the pork tenderloin, cutting most of the way through. (The two parts should still be attached.) Cover the meat with a piece of wax paper and pound the tenderloin with a kitchen mallet or rolling pin until it is thin enough to roll, no more than 1 inch thick. (If the tenderloin is thick, make two slits, one slit one-third of the way in on one side and the second slit one-third of the way in on the opposite side, then gently pull the sides out to lay it flat and pound it.)

4. Spread the spinach mixture down the center of the tenderloin, making a rectangle and leaving at least a 1-inch border on all sides. Roll the tenderloin lengthwise so it resembles a log. Secure it with toothpicks or kitchen twine so it holds together while cooking.

5. In a large ovenproof skillet, heat the remaining 2 teaspoons of the grapeseed oil over medium-high heat. Sprinkle the rolled tenderloin with the remaining ¼ teaspoon of pepper and place the tenderloin in the skillet. Sear it on all sides, then place the skillet in the oven and roast until the pork reaches an internal temperature of 145°F, 20 to 30 minutes. (When checking the temperature, make sure you are getting the temperature of the meat and not the stuffing. Place the thermometer in the center of the pork tenderloin and gently push it into the center of the roll. When you feel a little resistance, push it in just slightly and wait for the temperature to register.)

6. Remove the tenderloin from the oven and set it on a cutting board to rest for 10 minutes. Cover with the pesto sauce and cut into 6 to 8 (1½-inch-thick) rolls to serve.

COOKING TIP: Butterflying is a technique that allows you to make a piece of meat an even thickness that's thin enough to stuff and roll. To save time, you can ask your butcher to do it for you.

PER SERVING: Calories: 321; Total fat: 18g; Saturated fat: 3g; Cholesterol: 76mg; Sodium: 251mg; Carbohydrates: 4g; Fiber: 2g; Sugar: 1g; Protein: 27g

Beef Tenderloin Tips with Mushrooms and Beets

Serves 2 **Prep Time:** 20 minutes **Cook Time:** 1 hour

This decadent recipe is the one to turn to when you have something to celebrate! Beet greens are sweeter than many other leafy greens and are full of brain-supporting antioxidants.

FOR THE BEETS

2 large beets, greens attached

1 orange, halved and cut into slices

1 teaspoon extra-virgin olive oil

½ cup thinly sliced leeks, rinsed well, white and light green parts

Freshly ground black pepper

⅛ teaspoon kosher salt ▶

TO MAKE THE BEETS

1. Preheat the oven to 425°F.

2. Lay 2 (5-by-5-inch) pieces of aluminum foil on a cutting board. Wash the beets and cut off the leaves and stems. Place each beet in the middle of a sheet of aluminum foil. Lay half the orange slices around each beet and pull the foil up around the beet and orange, gathering it tightly around the stem. Place the beets on one side of a rimmed baking sheet and roast for 1 hour.

3. While the beets are roasting, in a medium saucepan over high heat, bring 4 cups of water to a boil. Wash the beet greens and stems well and cut them into 2-inch pieces. Add them to the boiling water and cook for 5 minutes, or until the stems are tender. Drain and set aside the cooked greens and stems.

4. Once the beets are tender, remove them from the oven, let them cool, and gently peel the skin off and dice them.

5. While the beets are cooling, in a small skillet, heat the olive oil over medium heat and sauté the leeks, beet greens, and stems for 3 to 5 minutes, until warmed through and the leeks are softened. Season with the salt and pepper.

FOR THE BEEF TIPS

2 teaspoons extra-virgin olive oil, divided

½ cup thinly sliced leeks, rinsed well, white and light green parts

8 ounces cremini mushrooms, sliced

8 ounces beef tenderloin tips, cut into 1-inch pieces

¼ teaspoon kosher salt

¼ teaspoon freshly ground black pepper

¼ cup red wine

TO MAKE THE BEEF TIPS

6. In a large heavy-bottomed skillet or cast-iron pan, heat 1 teaspoon of olive oil over medium heat. Add the leeks and mushrooms and cook for about 5 minutes, until softened. Remove the mixture from the skillet and set aside.

7. Increase the heat to medium-high. Season the tenderloin tips with salt and pepper. Heat 1 teaspoon of olive oil in the skillet, add the tenderloin tips, and sear them for about 5 minutes per side.

8. Add the wine and the leek-mushroom mixture. Stir to combine. Let it simmer for 5 minutes, until a sauce has formed and the meat is cooked to an internal temperature of 145°F.

9. Serve with roasted red potatoes and the beets and beet greens on the side.

VARIATION TIP: Filet tips are the ends of a tenderloin and often sold for a lower cost than filet mignon. If you can't find tenderloin tips or want to treat yourself, you can certainly substitute with filet mignon.

PER SERVING: Calories: 492; Total fat: 28g; Saturated fat: 11g; Cholesterol: 79mg; Sodium: 446mg; Carbohydrates: 28g; Fiber: 5g; Sugar: 15g; Protein: 26g

Grilled Pork Chops with Blueberry Barbecue Sauce

Serves 2 **Prep Time:** 15 minutes **Cook Time:** 50 minutes

The star of the show here is the blueberry barbecue sauce—you will get a healthy dose of brain-boosting blueberries in this sweet and smoky sauce!

FOR THE SAUCE

1 teaspoon extra-virgin olive oil

1 tablespoon finely chopped sweet onion

1 cup fresh or frozen blueberries

1 tablespoon apple cider vinegar

½ teaspoon Worcestershire sauce

⅛ teaspoon smoked paprika

¼ teaspoon chili powder

1½ tablespoons maple syrup

⅛ teaspoon kosher salt ▶

TO MAKE THE SAUCE

1. In a small saucepan, heat the olive oil over low heat, then add the onion and sauté for 3 minutes.

2. Increase the heat to medium-low, then add the blueberries, apple cider vinegar, Worcestershire sauce, paprika, chili powder, maple syrup, and salt and cook until the blueberries pop, about 5 minutes. Reduce the heat to low and simmer for about 30 minutes, or until the sauce thickens.

3. Let the sauce cool, then transfer it to a food processor and puree until it is mostly smooth. Set aside.

4. The sauce can be stored in an airtight container in the refrigerator for up to 1 week or in the freezer for up to 1 month.

TO MAKE THE PORK CHOPS

5. Heat the grill to 450°F.

6. Brush the pork chops with the oil and season both sides with salt and pepper.

FOR THE PORK CHOPS

2 (5-ounce) boneless pork
chops

1 teaspoon grapeseed oil
or avocado oil

Salt

Freshly ground black
pepper

7. Grill the pork chops for about 5 minutes on one side, then flip them over. Grill the pork chops on the other side for 5 minutes, or until the pork reaches an internal temperature of 145°F in the center.

8. Serve with half the blueberry barbecue sauce and some grilled vegetables on the side.

USE IT AGAIN: You can double the barbecue sauce and use it over grilled chicken later in the week.

PER SERVING: Calories: 305; Total fat: 10g; Saturated fat: 2g; Cholesterol: 94mg; Sodium: 252mg; Carbohydrates: 21g; Fiber: 2g; Sugar: 17g; Protein: 32g

CHAPTER 7

Snacks and Desserts

Hummus with Crudité and Pita Chips

Makes 2 cups of hummus **Prep Time:** 10 minutes

Filled with protein and healthy fats, hummus is a versatile snack. Add roasted red peppers or a swirl of pesto, or top it with sautéed mushrooms for a twist. You can add more or less garlic to suit your taste. I add a bit of salt to this dish because it really balances the flavor, but you can eliminate it and season the hummus with some added parsley, oregano, and an extra squeeze of lemon juice. Lemon juice is a good flavor enhancer and helps reduce the amount of salt needed.

1 (16-ounce) can chickpeas, drained and rinsed

2 large garlic cloves, peeled

½ cup tahini

2 tablespoons freshly squeezed lemon juice

⅓ cup extra-virgin olive oil

⅛ teaspoon kosher salt

Carrot sticks

Celery sticks

Grape tomatoes

Cucumber spears

Pita chips

Crackers

1. In the bowl of a food processor, place the chickpeas, garlic, tahini, and lemon juice. Pulse until well combined.

2. With the processor running, slowly pour the olive oil through the feed tube and process until smooth. Season with the salt.

3. Serve the hummus with carrot sticks, celery sticks, tomatoes, cucumber spears, pita chips, and crackers.

USE IT AGAIN: Use the leftover hummus in the Hummus and Vegetable Wrap (page 41) or serve it with Chicken Shawarma (page 82). It is also delicious spread on toast for a filling breakfast.

PER SERVING (½ CUP HUMMUS PLUS VEGETABLES): Calories: 419; Total fat: 35g; Saturated fat: 5g; Cholesterol: 0mg; Sodium: 234mg; Carbohydrates: 20g; Fiber: 6g; Sugar: 3g; Protein: 9g

Orange-Chocolate Date and Oat Energy Balls

Makes 6 energy balls **Prep Time:** 1 hour and 10 minutes

Dates are a sweet, partially dried fruit that are native to the Middle East. I love to use them to lend a bit of sweetness to a dish without adding a lot of refined sugar. They are full of antioxidants and may help reduce inflammation and the buildup of amyloid protein plaques in the brain. Soaking the dates in orange juice gives these bites a mild orange flavor, but don't soak them too long or they will become soggy.

½ cup chopped dates

¼ cup orange juice

½ cup old-fashioned oats

2 teaspoons dark unsweetened cocoa powder

1½ teaspoons confectioners' sugar

½ teaspoon orange zest

2 ounces toasted walnuts, chopped

1. In a small bowl, soak the dates in orange juice for 1 hour.

2. Drain any extra liquid from the dates and place the dates in the bowl of a food processor. Add the oats, cocoa powder, sugar, and orange zest and process until well combined.

3. Form the mixture into 6 balls. In a small bowl, place the walnuts. Roll the balls in the walnuts to coat them.

4. Store in an airtight container for up to 3 days at room temperature, up to 1 week in the refrigerator, or up to 2 months in the freezer.

VARIATION TIP: These energy balls are also delicious when rolled in toasted coconut or a mix of cocoa powder and confectioners' sugar.

PER SERVING (3 BALLS): Calories: 139; Total fat: 7g; Saturated fat: 1g; Cholesterol: 0mg; Sodium: 1mg; Carbohydrates: 18g; Fiber: 3g; Sugar: 10g; Protein: 3g

No-Bake Granola Bites

Makes 4 bites **Prep Time:** 10 minutes

Packaged granola bars are nice to have on hand, but they are typically full of sugar and fat. Making your own at home is easy and helps keep the fat and sugar content under control. I use maple syrup for its flavor and ability to hold the bar together, but it also adds antioxidants and minerals like magnesium and potassium, nutrients you can't get from refined sweeteners.

¼ cup chopped dates

½ cup low-fat granola

2 tablespoons creamy peanut butter

1 tablespoon pure maple syrup

1 teaspoon vanilla (optional)

1. In a small bowl, mix together the dates and granola. In a separate small bowl, mix together the peanut butter, maple syrup, and vanilla (if using) until it is a smooth, pourable consistency. Drizzle over the granola and dates and mix until the granola and dates are coated with the peanut butter mixture.

2. Divide the mixture into quarters. With damp hands, press each quarter of the mixture into a 1½-inch-by-2 ½-inch log that is about 1 inch thick.

3. You can wrap the bites individually in wax paper or store them in an airtight container for up to 1 week in the refrigerator or up to 2 months in the freezer.

VARIATION TIP: Add small dark chocolate chips to the mix for a little variety and sweetness.

PER SERVING (1 BITE): Calories: 136; Total fat: 5g; Saturated fat: 1g; Cholesterol: 0mg; Sodium: 63mg; Carbohydrates: 22g; Fiber: 3g; Sugar: 12g; Protein: 4g

Triple-Berry Nice Cream

Serves 2 **Prep Time:** 5 minutes

"Nice cream" is a delicious frozen treat. This homemade vegan dessert is sweet and refreshing and smooth like ice cream but without the fat. Freeze any extra berries you have on hand, then pull them out when you are ready for a treat. With all the berries in this recipe, you'll get a day's worth of brain-boosting fruit in one serving! Bananas are the key to making a nice cream, but you can swap the berries with any frozen fruit you like. Cherries or mangos taste delicious, or add a little dark chocolate cocoa powder for extra decadence.

1 cup frozen banana
  pieces

½ cup frozen diced
  strawberries

¼ cup frozen blackberries

¼ cup frozen blueberries

2 tablespoons
  almond milk

½ teaspoon vanilla

1. In the bowl of a food processor or high-powered blender, place the banana, strawberries, blackberries, and blueberries.

2. Pulse for 10 to 15 seconds to break down the ingredients. Then, with the processor running, pour the almond milk and vanilla through the feed tube and process for about 2 minutes, stopping every 20 to 30 seconds to scrape the sides down, until smooth.

3. Enjoy right away. Or you can store in an airtight container in the freezer for up to 2 weeks.

COOKING TIP: If the bananas and berries are frozen solid, allow them to sit in the processor for 5 minutes to thaw slightly before blending.

PER SERVING (¾ CUP): Calories: 149; Total fat: 1g; Saturated fat: 0g; Cholesterol: 0mg; Sodium: 9mg; Carbohydrates: 36g; Fiber: 6g; Sugar: 20g; Protein: 2g

Blueberry Peach Cobblers

Makes 2 cobblers **Prep Time:** 10 minutes **Cook Time:** 20 minutes

Blueberries have one of the highest antioxidant levels of all fruits and have been linked to slower rates of cognitive decline, but you'll only be thinking about how delicious they are as you enjoy this fruit-filled dessert.

1 cup fresh blueberries

2 small fresh peaches, pitted and diced

1 teaspoon lemon zest

1 teaspoon freshly squeezed lemon juice

¼ cup old-fashioned oats

1 tablespoon whole wheat flour

1 tablespoon lightly packed light brown sugar

¼ teaspoon cinnamon

¼ teaspoon nutmeg

2 teaspoons cold unsalted butter

1. Preheat the oven to 350°F. Place 2 (1-cup) ramekins on a rimmed baking sheet.

2. In a small bowl, combine the blueberries, peaches, lemon zest, and lemon juice and mix well. Divide the mixture evenly between the ramekins.

3. In another small bowl, mix the oats, flour, brown sugar, cinnamon, and nutmeg. Using clean hands, quickly work the butter into the oat mixture until it is evenly dispersed and the mixture is slightly crumbly. Spoon half the mixture over each of the fruit-filled ramekins. It will be mounded, but don't worry: the fruit will cook down, and it will perfectly fill the ramekin.

4. Place the baking sheet with the ramekins on a rack in the middle of the oven and bake for 20 minutes, just until the fruit mixture is bubbling. Transfer to a wire rack to cool slightly, then serve.

VARIATION TIP: For a vegan and dairy-free version, you can leave out the butter. The topping will be slightly drier but still delicious. If you don't have fresh blueberries or peaches, frozen will work just fine.

PER SERVING (1 COBBLER): Calories: 230; Total fat: 6g; Saturated fat: 3g; Cholesterol: 10mg; Sodium: 34mg; Carbohydrates: 43g; Fiber: 6g; Sugar: 25g; Protein: 5g

Grilled Pineapple Sundaes

Makes 2 sundaes **Prep Time:** 10 minutes **Cook Time:** 10 minutes

The sweet acidic bite from the pineapple brings out the rich cocoa flavor of the dark chocolate in this amazing combination. A little dark chocolate every day may be good for your brain—and no, you aren't imagining it if you feel like you got a mood boost after enjoying a piece. Some studies have shown that the flavonoids in dark chocolate may help stimulate areas in the brain that are responsible for mood. The higher the percentage of cocoa, the better. I use a chocolate bar that is at least 70 percent cacao, which helps limit the amount of sugar but still provides a bit of a sweet flavor.

4 (½-inch-thick) fresh pineapple rings

Avocado oil or cooking spray

1 cup vanilla frozen yogurt

1 ounce dark chocolate, melted

2 tablespoons chopped pistachios

1. Preheat the grill to 400°F or heat a grill pan over medium-high heat.

2. Brush each side of the pineapple slices with avocado oil. Place them on the hot grill and cook for 3 to 4 minutes per side, until the pineapple starts to brown and caramelize and easily pulls away from the grill. Remove the pineapple and set two rings aside. Cut the remaining rings into 2-inch pieces.

3. Place one pineapple ring on each of two plates. Add ½ cup frozen yogurt in the center of each ring. Top each with half the pineapple pieces and drizzle it with half the melted chocolate and sprinkle with 1 tablespoon of pistachios.

COOKING TIP: Cook the pineapple on the grill while you are grilling dinner. Set it aside and reheat it quickly in the microwave before serving.

PER SERVING (1 SUNDAE): Calories: 300; Total fat: 14g; Saturated fat: 6g; Cholesterol: 2mg; Sodium: 67mg; Carbohydrates: 41g; Fiber: 3g; Sugar: 35g; Protein: 6g

Dessert Charcuterie Board with Chocolate Hummus

Serves 4 **Prep Time:** 20 minutes

Charcuterie boards don't have to be full of cheese and salty meats. I love to have a little fun with dessert, and I built this charcuterie board around a dark chocolate hummus and homemade cinnamon pita chips. Although most of the recipes in this book are portioned for two, sometimes it's nice to have a dessert to share, and you can make this one as small or large as you like. It is perfect for a book club or a get-together with friends or family. If you want to size it down to feed just two people, enjoy the hummus and pita chips with strawberries on the side.

FOR THE CHOCOLATE HUMMUS

1 cup canned chickpeas, drained and rinsed

¼ cup tahini

2 tablespoons dark unsweetened cocoa powder

4 tablespoons maple syrup

¼ teaspoon kosher salt

FOR THE CINNAMON PITA CHIPS

½ teaspoon cinnamon

½ teaspoon sugar

1 (6-inch) pita bread

½ teaspoon extra-virgin olive oil ▶

TO MAKE THE CHOCOLATE HUMMUS

1. In the bowl of a food processor, place the chickpeas, tahini, cocoa powder, maple syrup, and salt and process until smooth and creamy.

2. Store the hummus in a tightly sealed container in the refrigerator until you are ready to build the charcuterie board. (It will keep for 3 to 4 days.)

TO MAKE THE CINNAMON PITA CHIPS

3. Preheat the oven to 425°F.

4. In a small bowl, combine the cinnamon and sugar.

5. Cut the pita bread in half and then separate each half into 2 pieces. Cut each side into 3 triangles. You will end up with 12 triangles.

6. Brush both sides of each triangle lightly with a little olive oil. Sprinkle all the triangles with the cinnamon-sugar mix.

FOR THE CHARCUTERIE BOARD

1 to 2 cups red and green grapes

6 to 8 fresh strawberries, cored and halved

½ Honeycrisp or Gala apple, sliced

2 or 3 figs, halved

¼ cup pistachios

¼ cup unsalted pecan halves

¼ cup yogurt-covered cranberries

Dark chocolate bars

Cranberry bread

7. Place the pita triangles on a baking sheet and place it in the preheated oven. Bake for 5 minutes, then flip the triangles and bake for 4 to 5 minutes more, or until they are browned and crispy.

8. Remove the pita triangles from the oven and cool on a wire rack.

TO BUILD THE CHARCUTERIE BOARD

9. Use a wooden cutting board or large serving platter or baking sheet covered with foil.

10. Place the grapes in the center of the board, then put the hummus in a small ramekin and place it on the board. Set the pita chips and rest of the ingredients decoratively around the board, mixing colors and textures.

VARIATION TIP: Build your board with a variety of brain-healthy fruits, nuts, and grains that you love, such as walnuts and pecans, blackberries, dates, red and purple grapes, and whole-grain crackers.

PER SERVING (¼ CUP HUMMUS AND 3 PITA CHIPS): Calories: 459; Total fat: 20g; Saturated fat: 4g; Cholesterol: 0mg; Sodium: 188mg; Carbohydrates: 66g; Fiber: 9g; Sugar: 36g; Protein: 11g

Lemony White Chocolate and Raspberry Mousse

Serves 2 **Prep Time:** 10 minutes, plus 3 hours to chill **Cook Time:** 2 minutes

Tofu is made from the curds of soy milk and is available in different textures, including silken, soft, and firm. Silken tofu has a very soft texture and is commonly used to make creamy sauces or to replace eggs in vegan recipes. In this recipe, the tofu replaces the heavy cream typically used in mousse recipes. Tofu contains less saturated fat than heavy cream and more protein, calcium, magnesium, and iron, adding some good nutrients to this dish.

2 ounces white chocolate chips

8 ounces silken tofu, drained

1 teaspoon lemon zest, plus more for garnish

1 tablespoon freshly squeezed lemon juice

1 tablespoon honey

½ cup fresh raspberries

Confectioners' sugar, for dusting (optional)

1. In a small microwave-safe bowl, place the white chocolate chips and microwave on high for 1 to 2 minutes, stirring every 30 seconds to melt the chips evenly.

2. In the bowl of a food processor, place the tofu, lemon zest, lemon juice, and honey and process until combined. Add the melted chocolate and process quickly.

3. Divide the mixture between two ramekins or dessert glasses and cover with plastic wrap. Place in the refrigerator for at least 3 hours or until set.

4. To serve, top each ramekin with ¼ cup of the raspberries. Garnish with a little lemon zest and confectioners' sugar (if using).

VARIATION TIP: Swap blueberries or blackberries for the raspberries, or use lime juice and zest in place of the lemon for a bright twist.

PER SERVING: Calories: 272; Total fat: 14g; Saturated fat: 6g; Cholesterol: 6mg; Sodium: 35mg; Carbohydrates: 32g; Fiber: 2g; Sugar: 28g; Protein: 10g

Dark Chocolate and Almond Mug Cakes

Serves 2 **Prep Time:** 10 minutes **Cook Time:** 2 minutes

I think every night after dinner my husband says, "I could really go for a piece of chocolate cake!" The beauty of these delicious dark chocolate mug cakes is that I can surprise him and pull them together while he is cleaning up from dinner, and they are the perfect portion for just the two of us. I use a little salt because it boosts the sweetness without adding more sugar.

½ cup all-purpose flour

3 tablespoons sugar

2 tablespoons dark unsweetened cocoa powder

1 teaspoon baking powder

⅛ teaspoon kosher salt

⅓ cup almond milk

2 tablespoons extra-virgin olive oil

1 teaspoon almond extract

Sliced strawberries

2 tablespoons chopped almonds

1. In a small bowl, whisk together the flour, sugar, cocoa powder, baking powder, and salt. In a measuring cup, mix the almond milk, olive oil, and almond extract. Whisk the wet ingredients into the dry ingredients until blended.

2. Divide the batter between 2 (10- to 12-ounce) coffee mugs. Place in the microwave and microwave on high for about 90 seconds, or until a toothpick comes out clean when inserted into the center of the cake.

3. Top each cake with half the sliced strawberries and 1 tablespoon of chopped almonds. You could also drizzle them with a little chocolate syrup for a special treat.

COOKING TIP: The cake may take an extra 10 to 30 seconds depending on how powerful the microwave is. Start at 90 seconds and check it; if it is too moist, put it back in the microwave for an extra 10 to 30 seconds.

PER SERVING: Calories: 368; Total fat: 17g; Saturated fat: 3g; Cholesterol: 1mg; Sodium: 181mg; Carbohydrates: 50g; Fiber: 3g; Sugar: 21g; Protein: 7g

CHAPTER 8

Staples

Pesto Sauce

Makes 1 cup **Prep Time:** 10 minutes

Although traditional pesto contains a healthy dose of Parmesan cheese, in this MIND diet–friendly version, I've left it out, making this sauce thinner than regular pesto. You can certainly add some cheese if you prefer. Basil and pine nuts are traditional ingredients, but arugula and walnuts also make a delicious pesto.

2 cups packed fresh basil leaves

1 tablespoon chopped garlic (about 2 large cloves)

2 teaspoons lemon zest

2 tablespoons freshly squeezed lemon juice

½ cup toasted pine nuts

½ cup extra-virgin olive oil

¼ teaspoon kosher salt

1. In the bowl of a food processor, place the basil, garlic, lemon zest, lemon juice, and pine nuts. Pulse until finely chopped.

2. With the processor running, slowly pour the olive oil through the feed tube and puree until the mixture is smooth. Add the salt and pulse quickly to combine.

3. Store in the refrigerator for up to 1 week, or freeze for up to 3 months.

USE IT AGAIN: To freeze, place 1 tablespoon of pesto in each well of an ice cube tray and freeze for up to 3 months. That way, you can pull out exactly how much you need when you are ready to use it.

PER SERVING (1 TABLESPOON): Calories: 90; Total fat: 10g; Saturated fat: 1g; Cholesterol: 0mg; Sodium: 20mg; Carbohydrates: 1g; Fiber: 0g; Sugar: 0g; Protein: 1g

Tahini Dressing

Makes ⅓ cup **Prep Time:** 5 minutes

Tahini is a staple in Mediterranean dishes, and it's often used to make dressings and sauces. Rich in monounsaturated fat and antioxidants that help reduce inflammation, this dressing can be added to salads, drizzled over hummus, or used as a dip for vegetables. It is delicious in Couscous Salad (page 82) or drizzled over Baked Falafel (page 54).

2 tablespoons tahini

1 teaspoon minced garlic

1 tablespoon freshly squeezed lemon juice

¼ teaspoon sugar

1 teaspoon white wine vinegar

¼ cup extra-virgin olive oil

1. In a small bowl, mix the tahini, garlic, lemon juice, sugar, and vinegar until well combined.

2. Slowly whisk in the olive oil and continue whisking until it is thoroughly combined.

3. Store in an airtight container in the refrigerator for up to 2 weeks.

COOKING TIP: Tahini is a paste made from toasted sesame seeds and has a slightly thinner consistency than peanut butter. You often have to stir the oil back into the paste before using it. Keep tahini in the refrigerator to preserve its flavor and to prevent it from spoiling.

PER SERVING (2 TABLESPOONS): Calories: 223; Total fat: 23g; Saturated fat: 3g; Cholesterol: 0mg; Sodium: 12mg; Carbohydrates: 3g; Fiber: 1g; Sugar: 1g; Protein: 2g

Spicy Avocado Dressing

Makes ¾ cup **Prep Time:** 10 minutes

This rich and spicy avocado dressing will add a creamy kick to salads, sandwiches, and tacos, and it is delicious spread on a slice of toast in the morning. You can adjust the spice level of the dressing by adjusting the amount of jalapeño pepper and garlic. Avocados are rich in monounsaturated fat and potassium, both of which are important for blood pressure control and may help improve blood flow to the brain.

1 medium ripe avocado, pitted, peeled, and diced

1 teaspoon lime zest

3 tablespoons freshly squeezed lime juice

1 tablespoon chopped jalapeño pepper

2 teaspoons chopped garlic (about 2 cloves)

2 tablespoons extra-virgin olive oil

1 tablespoon chopped fresh cilantro

1 tablespoon chopped fresh parsley

1. In the bowl of a food processor, place the avocado, lime zest, lime juice, jalapeño pepper, garlic, olive oil, cilantro, and parsley. Process until completely combined and no large pieces of avocado, cilantro, or parsley are visible.

2. Store in an airtight container in the refrigerator for up to 1 week. The lime juice will keep the dressing from turning brown.

USE IT AGAIN: Make a batch of this dressing to use throughout the week on tacos, a Salmon Breakfast Sandwich (page 28), Sheet-Pan Chicken Fajitas (page 80), or Sesame-Ginger Shrimp Sliders (page 66).

PER SERVING (2 TABLESPOONS): Calories: 100; Total fat: 9g; Saturated fat: 1g; Cholesterol: 0mg; Sodium: 4mg; Carbohydrates: 5g; Fiber: 2g; Sugar: 1g; Protein: 1g

Homemade Vegetable Broth

Makes 4 cups **Prep Time:** 10 minutes **Cook Time:** 2 to 3 hours

Making your own vegetable broth is a good way to use up vegetable scraps, cutting down on food waste. I keep a bag of vegetable scraps in my freezer and make a batch every few weeks. It is easy to put a pot on the stove and let it cook all afternoon. Your house will smell wonderful, and you will have it to use throughout the week. This broth is unsalted so you can adjust the seasoning in the dishes you'll use it in later. For the assorted vegetables, I recommend celery, carrots, onion, potatoes, and leek tops. If you want to pass on the starch, skip the potatoes.

2 pounds assorted
  vegetables

6 cups cold water

½ tablespoon black
  peppercorns

2 fresh thyme sprigs

2 fresh parsley sprigs

VARIATION TIP: It is also a great base for making chicken or beef stock. Add chicken or beef bones to the vegetable mixture (don't include the potatoes) and follow the same process.

1. Cut the vegetables into 2- to 3-inch pieces.

2. Place the vegetable pieces in a stockpot. Cover with the cold water.

3. Tie up the peppercorns, thyme, and parsley in a piece of cheesecloth and place it in the water.

4. Bring the water to a boil over high heat, then reduce the heat to low and simmer, covered, for 2 to 3 hours.

5. Let the broth cool slightly, then strain it, removing the vegetable pieces and the cheesecloth with the herbs.

6. Place the broth in two or three separate containers, cool, then store in the refrigerator for up to 5 days. The broth keeps in the freezer for up to 4 months.

PER SERVING (½ CUP): Calories: 10; Total fat: 0g; Saturated fat: 0g; Cholesterol: 0mg; Sodium: 7mg; Carbohydrates: 5g; Fiber: 0g; Sugar: 2g; Protein: 0g

Zesty Tomato Sauce

Makes 1½ cups **Prep Time:** 5 minutes **Cook Time:** 15 minutes

Plain canned tomato sauces will work in most dishes, but most store-bought tomato sauces are high in sodium. I use this sauce as a base and adjust it to match the dish I'm making. Basil, oregano, and red pepper flakes are good additions for a spicy Italian dish, or add some cumin and chili powder for a southwestern dish. If you can't find tomato puree, crushed tomatoes will work as well.

1 teaspoon extra-virgin olive oil

2 teaspoons finely chopped sweet onion

1 teaspoon minced garlic

1 (15-ounce) can no-salt added tomato puree

1. In a medium skillet, heat the olive oil over medium heat. Add the onion and sauté until just softened, 5 to 10 minutes. Add the garlic and cook for 1 minute.

2. Reduce the heat to medium-low, then pour in the tomato puree and cook for about 5 minutes, until thickened. Remove from the heat.

3. If you aren't using it right away, transfer the sauce to a small airtight container. Store in the refrigerator for up to 5 days or in the freezer for 4 to 6 months.

USE IT AGAIN: Mix any leftover sauce into sautéed zucchini and summer squash for an easy side dish.

PER SERVING (¼ CUP SAUCE): Calories: 20; Total fat: 1g; Saturated fat: 0g; Cholesterol: 0mg; Sodium: 8mg; Carbohydrates: 3g; Fiber: 1g; Sugar: 2g; Protein: 1g

Southwest Seasoning Blend

Makes 3 tablespoons **Prep Time:** 5 minutes

Premade taco seasoning blends tend to be high in sodium, so it's best to make your own so you can skip the salt entirely. This blend will keep for up to a year in a tightly sealed jar in the pantry. It is delicious in Tilapia Fish Tacos (page 62), Sheet-Pan Chicken Fajitas (page 80), and Stuffed Banana Peppers (page 53).

2 teaspoons ground cumin

1¼ teaspoons chili powder

½ teaspoon smoked paprika

1 teaspoon garlic powder

1 teaspoon onion powder

1¼ teaspoons dried Mexican oregano

1¼ teaspoons dried parsley

½ teaspoon freshly ground black pepper

In a small bowl, whisk together the cumin, chili powder, paprika, garlic powder, onion powder, oregano, parsley, and pepper. Store in a tightly sealed jar in the pantry for up to 1 year.

COOKING TIP: Humidity, hot temperatures, and light will cause your spices to lose their pungency quickly. Store all dried spices in a cool, dark cabinet, away from the stove, and always measure them out before you start cooking.

PER SERVING (½ TEASPOON): Calories: 3; Total fat: 0g; Saturated fat: 0g; Cholesterol: 0mg; Sodium: 6mg; Carbohydrates: 1g; Fiber: 0g; Sugar: 0g; Protein: 0g

Measurements and Conversions

VOLUME EQUIVALENTS	U.S. STANDARD	U.S. STANDARD (OUNCES)	METRIC (APPROXIMATE)
LIQUID	2 tablespoons	1 fl. oz.	30 mL
	¼ cup	2 fl. oz.	60 mL
	½ cup	4 fl. oz.	120 mL
	1 cup	8 fl. oz.	240 mL
	1½ cups	12 fl. oz.	355 mL
	2 cups or 1 pint	16 fl. oz.	475 mL
	4 cups or 1 quart	32 fl. oz.	1 L
	1 gallon	128 fl. oz.	4 L
DRY	⅛ teaspoon		0.5 mL
	¼ teaspoon		1 mL
	½ teaspoon		2 mL
	¾ teaspoon		4 mL
	1 teaspoon		5 mL
	1 tablespoon		15 mL
	¼ cup		59 mL
	⅓ cup		79 mL
	½ cup		118 mL
	⅔ cup		156 mL
	¾ cup		177 mL
	1 cup		235 mL
	2 cups or 1 pint		475 mL
	3 cups		700 mL
	4 cups or 1 quart		1 L
	½ gallon		2 L
	1 gallon		4 L

OVEN TEMPERATURES

FAHRENHEIT	CELSIUS (APPROXIMATE)
250°F	120°C
300°F	150°C
325°F	165°C
350°F	180°C
375°F	190°C
400°F	200°C
425°F	220°C
450°F	230°C

WEIGHT EQUIVALENTS

U.S. STANDARD	METRIC (APPROXIMATE)
½ ounce	15 g
1 ounce	30 g
2 ounces	60 g
4 ounces	115 g
8 ounces	225 g
12 ounces	340 g
16 ounces or 1 pound	455 g

References

Agarwal, Puja, Thomas M. Holland, Yamin Wang, David A. Bennett, and Martha Clare Morris. "Association of Strawberries and Anthocyanidin Intake with Alzheimer's Dementia Risk." *Nutrients* 11, no. 12 (2019): 3060. DOI.org/10.3390/nu11123060.

Bekdash, Rola A. "Choline, the Brain and Neurodegeneration: Insights from Epigenetics." *Frontiers in Bioscience-Landmark* 23, no. 6 (2018): 1113–43. DOI.org/10.2741/4636.

Böhm, Volker, Georg Lietz, Begoña Olmedilla-Alonso, David Phelan, Emmanuelle Reboul, Diana Bánati, Patrick Borel, et al. "From Carotenoid Intake to Carotenoid Blood and Tissue Concentrations—Implications for Dietary Intake Recommendations." *Nutrition Reviews* 79, no. 5 (May 2021): 544–73. DOI.org/10.1093/nutrit/nuaa008.

Chauhan, Abha, and Ved Chauhan. "Beneficial Effects of Walnuts on Cognition and Brain Health." *Nutrients* 12, no. 2 (February 2020): 550. DOI.org/10.3390/nu12020550.

Chew, Hannah, Victoria A. Solomon, and Alfred N. Fonteh. "Involvement of Lipids in Alzheimer's Disease Pathology and Potential Therapies." *Frontiers in Physiology* 11 (June 2020): 598. DOI.org/10.3389/fphys.2020.00598.

Devore, Elizabeth E., Jae Hee Kang, Monique M. B. Breteler, and Francine Grodstein. "Dietary Intake of Berries and Flavonoids in Relation to Cognitive Decline." *Annals of Neurology* 72, no. 1 (July 2012): 135–43. DOI.org/10.1002/ana.23594.

Dhana, Klodian, Denis A. Evans, Kumar B. Rajan, David A. Bennett, and Martha C. Morris. "Healthy Lifestyle and the Risk of Alzheimer Dementia: Findings from 2 Longitudinal Studies." *Neurology* 95 no. 4 (July 2020): e374–83. DOI.org/10.1212/WNL.0000000000009816.

Duplantier, Sally C., and Christopher D. Gardner. "A Critical Review of the Study of Neuroprotective Diets to Reduce Cognitive Decline." *Nutrients* 13, no. 7 (2021): 2264. DOI.org/10.3390/nu13072264.

Echouffo-Tcheugui, Justin B., Sarah C. Conner, Jayandra J. Himali, Pauline Maillard, Charles S. DeCarli, Alexa S. Beiser, Ramachandran S. Vasan, and Sudha Seshadri. "Circulating Cortisol and Cognitive and Structural Brain Measures: The Framingham Heart Study." *Neurology* 91 no. 21 (November 2018): e1961–70. DOI.org/10.1212/WNL.0000000000006549.

Fernandes, Iva, Rosa Pérez-Gregorio, Susana Soares, Nuno Mateus, and Victor de Freitas. "Wine Flavonoids in Health and Disease Prevention." *Molecules* 22, no. 2 (2017): 292. DOI.org/10.3390/molecules22020292.

Grimmig, Bethany, Seol-Hee Kim, Kevin Nash, Paula C. Bickford, and R. Douglas Shytle. "Neuroprotective Mechanisms of Astaxanthin: A Potential Therapeutic Role in Preserving Cognitive Function in Age and Neurodegeneration." *GeroScience* 39, no. 1 (February 2017): 19–32. DOI.org/10.1007/s11357-017-9958-x.

Jardim, Fernanda Rafaela, Fernando Tonon de Rossi, Marielle Xavier Nascimento, Renata Gabriele da Silva Barros, Paula Agrizzi Borges, Isabella Cristina Prescilio, and Marcos Roberto de Oliveira. "Resveratrol and Brain Mitochondria: A Review." *Molecular Neurobiology* 55, no. 3 (March 2018): 2085–101. DOI.org/10.1007/s12035-017-0448-z.

Karama, S., S. Ducharme, J. Corley, F. Chouinard-Decorte, J. M. Starr, J. M. Wardlaw, M. E. Bastin, and I. J. Deary. "Cigarette Smoking and Thinning of the Brain's Cortex." *Molecular Psychiatry* 20 (2015): 778–85. DOI.org/10.1038/mp.2014.187.

Klimova, Blanka, Kamil Kuca, Martin Valis, and Jakub Hort. "Role of Nut Consumption in the Management of Cognitive Decline—A Mini-Review." *Current Alzheimer Research* 15, no. 9 (2018): 877–82. DOI.org/10.2174/1567205015666180202100721.

Kulashekar, Malavvika, Sayra M. Stom, and Jacob D. Peuler. "Resveratrol's Potential in the Adjunctive Management of Cardiovascular Disease, Obesity, Diabetes, Alzheimer Disease, and Cancer." *Journal of the American Osteopathic Association* 118, no. 9 (September 2018): 596–605. DOI.org/10.7556/jaoa.2018.133.

Lee, Yoon-Mi, Sang-Ik Han, Byeng Chun Song, and Kyung-Jin Yeum. "Bioactives in Commonly Consumed Cereal Grains: Implications for Oxidative Stress and Inflammation." *Journal of Medicinal Food* 18, no. 11 (November 2015): 1179–86. DOI.org/10.1089/jmf.2014.3394.

Liu, Kai, Suocheng Hui, Bin Wang, Kanakaraju Kaliannan, Xiaozhong Guo, and Linlang Liang. "Comparative Effects of Different Types of Tree Nut Consumption on Blood Lipids: A Network Meta-analysis of Clinical Trials." *American Journal of Clinical Nutrition* 111, no. 1 (January 2020): 219–27. DOI.org/10.1093/ajcn/nqz280.

Lu, Yanhui, Yu An, Chenyan Lv, Weiwei Ma, Yuandi Xi, and Rong Xiao. "Dietary Soybean Isoflavones in Alzheimer's Disease Prevention." *Asia Pacific Journal of Clinical Nutrition* 27, no. 5 (2018): 946–54. DOI.org/10.6133/apjcn.052018.01.

Monacelli, Fiammetta, Erica Acquarone, Chiara Giannotti, Roberta Borghi, and Alessio Nencioni. "Vitamin C, Aging and Alzheimer's Disease." *Nutrients* 9, no. 7 (July 2017): 670. DOI.org/10.3390/nu9070670.

Morris, Martha Clare, Christy C. Tangney, Yamin Wang, Frank M. Sacks, David A. Bennett, Neelum T. Aggarwal. "MIND Diet Associated with Reduced Incidence of Alzheimer's Disease." *Alzheimer's & Dementia* 11, no. 9 (2015): 1007–14. DOI.org/10.1016/j.jalz.2014.11.009.

Morris, Martha Clare, Christy C. Tangney, Yamin Wang, Frank M. Sacks, Lisa L. Barnes, David A. Bennett, and Neelum T. Aggarwal. "MIND Diet Slows Cognitive Decline with Aging." *Alzheimer's & Dementia* 11, no. 9 (2015): 1015–22. DOI.org/10.1016/j.jalz.2015.04.011.

Morris, Martha Clare, Yamin Wang, Lisa L. Barnes, David A. Bennett, Bess Dawson-Hughes, and Sarah L. Booth. "Nutrients and Bioactives in Green Leafy Vegetables and Cognitive Decline." *Neurology* 90, no. 3 (January 16, 2018): e214–22. DOI.org/10.1212/WNL.0000000000004815.

Mullins, Amy P., and Bahram H. Arjmandi. "Health Benefits of Plant-Based Nutrition: Focus on Beans in Cardiometabolic Diseases." *Nutrients* 13, no. 2 (February 2021): 519. DOI.org/10.3390/nu13020519.

Opie, R. S., C. Itsiopoulos, N. Parletta, A. Sanchez-Villegas, T. N. Akbaraly, A. Ruusunen, and F. N. Jacka. "Dietary Recommendations for the Prevention of Depression." *Nutritional Neuroscience* 20, no. 3 (2017): 161–71. DOI.org/10.1179/1476830515Y.0000000043.

Panche, A. N., A. D. Diwan, and S. R. Chandra. "Flavonoids: An Overview." *Journal of Nutritional Science* 5 (December 2016): e47. DOI.org/10.1017/jns.2016.41.

Pistollato, Francesca, Ruben Calderón Iglesias, Roberto Ruiz, Silvia Aparicio, Jorge Crespo, Luis Dzul Lopez, Piera Pia Manna, et al. "Nutritional Patterns Associated with the Maintenance of Neurocognitive Functions and the Risk of Dementia and Alzheimer's Disease: A Focus on Human Studies." *Pharmacological Research* 131 (2018): 32–43. DOI.org/10.1016/j.phrs.2018.03.012.

Rajaram, Sujatha, Julie Jones, and Grace J. Lee. "Plant-Based Dietary Patterns, Plant Foods, and Age-Related Cognitive Decline." *Advances in Nutrition* 10, no. S4 (2019): S422–36. DOI.org/10.1093/advances/nmz081.

Rusu, Marius Emil, Andrei Mocan, Isabel C. F. R. Ferreira, and Daniela-Saventa Popa. "Health Benefits of Nut Consumption in Middle-Aged and Elderly Population." *Antioxidants* 8, no. 8 (August 2019): 302. DOI.org/10.3390/antiox8080302.

Samieri, Cécilia, Martha-Clare Morris, David A. Bennett, Claudine Berr, Philippe Amouyel, Jean-François Dartigues, Christophe Tzourio, et al. "Fish Intake, Genetic Predisposition to Alzheimer Disease, and Decline in Global Cognition and Memory in 5 Cohorts of Older Persons." *American Journal of Epidemiology* 187, no. 5 (May 2018): 933–40. DOI.org/10.1093/aje/kwx330.

Smith, A. David, Helga Refsum, Teodoro Bottiglieri, Michael Fenech, Babak Hooshmand, Andrew McCaddon, Joshua W. Miller, et al. "Homocysteine and Dementia: An International Consensus Statement." *Journal of Alzheimer's Disease* 62, no. 2 (2018): 561–70. DOI.org/10.3233/JAD-171042.

Thomas, J., C. J. Thomas, J. Radcliffe, and C. Itsiopoulos. "Omega-3 Fatty Acids in Early Prevention of Inflammatory Neurodegenerative Disease: A Focus on Alzheimer's Disease." *Biomed Research International* 2015 (2015): 172801. DOI.org/10.1155/2015/172801.

van den Brink, Annelien C., Elske M. Brouwer-Brolsma, Agnes A. M. Berendsen, and Ondine van de Rest. "The Mediterranean, Dietary Approaches to Stop Hypertension (DASH), and Mediterranean-DASH Intervention for Neurodegenerative Delay (MIND) Diets Are Associated with Less Cognitive Decline and a Lower Risk of Alzheimer's Disease—A Review." *Advances in Nutrition* 10, no. 6 (November 2019): 1040–65. DOI.org/10.1093/advances/nmz054.

Volpe, Stella Lucia. "Magnesium in Disease Prevention and Overall Health." *Advances in Nutrition* 4, no. 3 (May 2013): 378S–83S. DOI.org/10.3945/an.112.003483.

Yu, Jin-Tai, Wei Xu, Chen-Chen Tan, Sandrine Andrieu, John Suckling, Evangelos Evangelou, An Pan, et al. (2020). "Evidence-Based Prevention of Alzheimer's Disease: Systematic Review and Meta-analysis of 243 Observational Prospective Studies and 153 Randomised Controlled Trials." *Journal of Neurology, Neurosurgery & Psychiatry* 91, no. 11 (2020): 1201–09. DOI.org/10.1136/jnnp-2019-321913.

Index

Page locators in **bold** indicate a picture

Acknowledgments

I would not have been able to write this without the love, support, and encouragement from my wonderful husband, Mark. Thank you for being open to trying so many things, listening to my crazy ideas, tasting everything I made, and washing all those dishes! Thank you to my parents for instilling in me a love for food and travel, curiosity, and a strong work ethic. To my brothers and sister, thank you for trying everything I made as we were growing up and encouraging me to keep cooking! I am so grateful to all my wonderful colleagues who have inspired me throughout my career and encouraged me to dive in, try new things, and do what I love. I'm especially thankful to Lisa Cicciarello Andrews, RD, for introducing me to the Callisto team and encouraging me throughout this process, and to my editor, Sierra Machado, for her thoughtful comments and guidance as I navigated this new challenge.

To all those with a family history of dementia and those caring for people with dementia, your dedication to your loved ones inspires me, and I hope you find a few things in this book that inspire you to make positive nutritional changes to protect your brain and your overall health.

About the Author

Laura Ali, MS, RDN, LDN, is a food-loving registered dietitian, culinary nutritionist, and freelance writer based in Pittsburgh, PA. Growing up, she loved spending time in the kitchen, grocery shopping, and experimenting with recipes and knew she had to do something with food in her professional life. With more than 30 years of food and nutrition experience, Laura specializes in working with consumers and health-focused companies, teaching simple, delicious ways to incorporate healthy foods into everyday meals. Laura is active in professional organizations, currently serving as the assistant editor of *Tastings*, the newsletter for the Food and Culinary Practice Group. She is a past president of the Pittsburgh Academy of Nutrition and Dietetics and recipient of both the Pennsylvania Academy of Nutrition and Dietetics Keystone Award and the Recognized Young Dietitian of the Year Award. This is her first cookbook. Follow her on Instagram and Twitter @LauraAli_RD and on her website, LauraMAli.com, where she shares delicious recipes and tips to make life easier in the kitchen.

Printed in the USA
CPSIA information can be obtained
at www.ICGtesting.com
CBHW041133270224
4709CB00002B/6